Emeril's

There's a Chef in My Family!

Recipes to Get Everybody Cooking

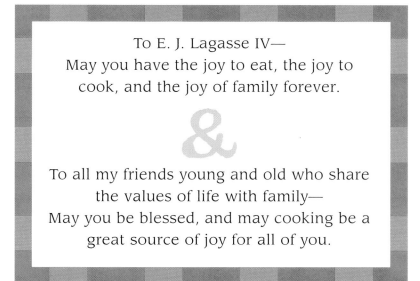

To E. J. Lagasse IV—
May you have the joy to eat, the joy to
cook, and the joy of family forever.

&

To all my friends young and old who share
the values of life with family—
May you be blessed, and may cooking be a
great source of joy for all of you.

ALSO BY EMERIL LAGASSE

From Emeril's Kitchens
(2003)

Emeril's There's a Chef in My Soup!
Recipes for the Kid in Everyone
(2002)

Prime Time Emeril
(2001)

Every Day's a Party
with Marcelle Bienvenu and Felicia Willett (1999)

Emeril's TV Dinners
with Marcelle Bienvenu and Felicia Willett (1998)

Emeril's Creole Christmas
with Marcelle Bienvenu (1997)

Louisiana Real & Rustic
with Marcelle Bienvenu (1996)

Emeril's New New Orleans Cooking
with Jessie Tirsch (1993)

—ACKNOWLEDGMENTS—

EMERIL'S THERE'S A CHEF IN MY FAMILY! would not have been possible without the love, hard work, and support from the following members of my extended family. My heartfelt thanks go out to every one of you:

- Miss Hilda and Mr. John, the best mom and dad ever, who taught me all I know about being part of a real family

- My beautiful wife, Alden, my daughters Jessie and Jillie, and my son, E. J., who give meaning to the word "family," and who are the light of my life

- Charlotte Armstrong Martory, for spearheading this very exciting project, for her incredible vision and commitment to this book, not to mention her love for kids and her amazing culinary skills—I thank you for keeping all of us on track. The Family Track!

- The Emeril's Culinary Team—Chef David McCelvey, Chef Bernard Carmouche, Marcelle Bienvenu, Charlotte Armstrong Martory, Trevor Wisdom, Alain Joseph, and Sarah O. Etheridge—whose taste buds, expertise, and tireless energy in the test kitchen make all of my projects come to life

- Marti Dalton, whose creativity never tires and who is always on the mark!

- Mara Warner, for her firm yet gentle management of all aspects of my life

- My compadres and supporters in matters great and small, Eric Linquest, Tony Cruz, and Mauricio Andrade

- Jim McGrew, for his expert legal counsel in all matters

- My Homebase family, for being my rock

- All the Homebase families who so graciously allowed their photographs to appear in this book—what a beautiful bunch of folks you are!

- My ever-growing restaurant family: Emeril's Restaurant, NOLA, and Emeril's Delmonico Restaurant in New Orleans; Emeril's New Orleans Fish House and Delmonico Steakhouse in Las Vegas; Emeril's Restaurant Orlando and Emeril's Tchoup Chop in Orlando; Emeril's Restaurant Atlanta; and Emeril's Restaurant Miami Beach, for making me one very proud father

- Melda LaChute, Julio Alejandro Yanes, and Megan Linquest, for sharing your delicious recipes with me!

- Photographer Quentin Bacon, whose eye always knows best, and his wonderful assistant, Amy Sims

- All the folks at HarperCollins Children's Books, who agree with me that there's a chef in every family and who committed themselves to making this cookbook into something very, very special:

  Susan Katz, Publisher; Kate Jackson, Senior V.P., Associate Publisher, and Editor-in-Chief; Toni Markiet, Executive Editor; Martha Rago, Executive Art Director; Tom Starace, Art Director; Robin Stamm, Editor; Meghan Dietsche, Editorial Assistant; Amelia Anderson, Design Assistant; Diane Naughton, V.P. of Marketing; Mary McAveney, Director of Hardcover Marketing; Amy Burton, Associate Director of Publicity; Carrie Bachman, Director of Publicity (Adult Division); Gypsy Lovett, Publicity Manager (Adult Division); Victoria Ingham, Director of Children's Online Marketing; John Vitale, V.P., Director of Production; Lucille Schneider, Associate Director of Production; Julie Blattberg, Managing Editor; Amy Vinchesi, Senior Production Editor; Laura Reese, Desktop Project Coordinator

- And to the creative genius of illustrator Charles Yuen, who once again has made a book into a feast for the eyes

Emeril's

There's a Chef in My Family!

Recipes to Get Everybody Cooking

CONTENTS

TAKING IT TO THE NEXT STEP 2

A GOOD COOK IS A SAFE COOK! 4

THE NUTS AND BOLTS 8

GOOD THINGS TO KNOW 14

BEAUTIFUL BEGINNINGS 27

IT'S-A-GOOD-MORNING MUFFINS 28

TOTALLY-FROM-SCRATCH BISCUITS 30

EGG-STRA SPECIAL OMELETS 32

EMERIL'S FAVORITE FRIED EGG SANDWICH 34

WAFFABLE WAFFLES 36

ONE-STOP BREAKFAST CASSEROLE 40

OOEY GOOEY BLUEBERRY "FRENCH TOAST" 42

DOUBLY DELICIOUS HOT CHOCOLATE WITH
  REAL WHIPPED CREAM 44

THE BREAD BOX 47

NEVER-ENOUGH DINNER ROLLS 48

YES-YOU-CAN BAGELS 50

HOT-OUT-OF-THE-OVEN BREAD 52

EVERYONE LOVES CORNBREAD 54

FOCACCIA, ANYONE? 56

TRY IT, YOU'LL LIKE IT ZUCCHINI BREAD 58

SENSATIONAL SALADS 61

CATCH A SHRIMP COCKTAIL 62

MY KINDA SALAD 64

POWER-PACKED SPINACH SALAD 66

BEANS GALORE SALAD 68

CHEF EMERIL'S SALAD 70

TALK ABOUT A TACO SALAD 72

SOUPER-DUPER SOUPS AND SANDWICHES 75

FEEL-GOOD CHICKEN AND RICE SOUP 76

HOT AND HEARTY MINESTRONE 78

TORTELLINI IN BRODO 80

PIZZAZY PIZZA SANDWICHES 82

FILL-'ER-UP FOCACCIA WITH ROASTED VEGGIES 84

OPEN-FACED ROAST TURKEY SANDWICHES 86

TOTALLY SLOPPY JOES 88

CHECK OUT MY CHICKEN SALAD SANDWICHES 90

SNACK ATTACK 93

NACHO FIESTA 94

BLOW-YOU-AWAY BAGEL CHIPS 98

OVEN CRISPY CHEESE FRIES 100

CHEESY PUFF PASTRY—WITH A TWIST 102

FONDUE FOR YOU 104

EMERIL'S CON QUESO 106

MMMM-HMMM HUMMUS 108

SCOOP-IT-UP SPINACH DIP 110

CONTENTS

TIME FOR DINNER! 113

VERY VEGGIE LASAGNA 114

FETTUCCINE ALFREDO MY WAY 116

PASTA PRIMAVERA 118

SAY "CHEESE" ENCHILADAS 120

GARLIC LOVERS' POT ROAST 122

MIGHTY MEATY MEATLOAF 124

PENNE WITH ITALIAN SAUSAGE 126

CRUNCHY CORN CHIP PIE 128

BREAD 'EM AND BAKE 'EM PORK CHOPS 130

SHEPHERD'S PIE 132

JUNIOR WELLINGTONS 134

CHICKEN PARMESAN EMERIL-STYLE 136

RAINY-DAY BBQ CHICKEN 138

PERFECT ROAST CHICKEN 140

CLASSIC ROAST TURKEY 142

FISH IN A POUCH 146

EMERIL'S FAVORITE STUFFED SHRIMP 148

MAMBO RICE "LASAGNA" 150

SIDES THAT SIZZLE 155

OVEN-ROASTED VEGGIES 156

CORN-OFF-THE-COB PUDDING 158

BEAN TOWN BAKED BEANS 160

REAL-DEAL RICE PILAF 162

SIMPLE-BUT-FABULOUS STUFFING 164

SUGAR-AND-SPICE ACORN SQUASH 166

SIMPLY DELICIOUS ARTICHOKES 168

BEST BAKED TOMATOES 170

MINTY GREEN PEAS 172

SWEET ENDINGS 175

MEGAN'S WHITE CHOCOLATE BARK WITH PECANS 176

PIECE-OF-THE-PIE PECAN BARS 178

BIG AND CHEWY OATMEAL COOKIES 180

BASICALLY BUTTERY COOKIES 182

MISS HILDA'S POPCORN CAKE 184

JUST-CHILLIN' CHOCOLATE FRIDGE PIE 186

LEMON ICEBOX PIE 188

VERY STRAWBERRY SHORTCAKE 190

NEW ORLEANS–STYLE BREAD PUDDING WITH CHOCOLATE SAUCE 192

HAZELNUTTY NUGGETS 194

CANDY-BAR-STUFFED BAKED APPLES 196

PURE AND SIMPLE CREAM PUFFS 198

MY FIRST WATERMELON GRANITA 202

Appendix 204

Index 206

Emeril's
There's a Chef in My Family!

Recipes to Get Everybody Cooking

TAKING IT TO THE NEXT STEP

WELCOME, FRIENDS! It has been one of my greatest missions in life to get people of all ages involved in cooking. It's creative, it's fun, and, best of all, it brings family and friends together. In my first cookbook for kids—EMERIL'S THERE'S A CHEF IN MY SOUP!: *Recipes for the Kid in Everyone*—I wanted to introduce younger folks to the basics of cooking. Now that we're all a little older, here is EMERIL'S THERE'S A CHEF IN MY FAMILY!: *Recipes to Get Everybody Cooking*. This book will help you take things to the next step.

We wrote this book with families in mind, as a way of getting everyone in the household into the kitchen. The recipes are a bit more complex, and kids may need more help with some of them, but we've really tried to include something for everyone. Whether you are younger or older, a beginner, intermediate, or professional cook, I think you will truly enjoy this new book. Even the youngest person in the house can help with simple stuff like tearing lettuce leaves or shucking corn, and I know those of you who are a little more experienced will continue to be excited by these recipes. Each one has something that anyone can do, and you'll learn to be creative with some old family favorites. Hey, if you want to see how a family can collaborate to create something special, check out Mambo Rice "Lasagna" on page 150. My young friend Julio Yanes took his grandmother Tessie's favorite meal of Cuban-style roast pork, beans and rice, and fried plantains and came up with a way to combine it into one super party dish. You see—cooking really is a family affair!

And after you cook together, with everyone pitching in along the way to make a meal that the whole family will enjoy, then you can sit down and eat! This was how it was done in my house when I was growing up, and this is what I am trying to get folks to go back to. Because if you ask me, one of the greatest joys of cooking is that it brings people together and makes them feel connected to one another. Over the past couple of years, and especially since EMERIL'S THERE'S A CHEF IN MY SOUP! was published, I've noticed that there are many kids out there who are not only helping in the kitchen, but who are *really* cooking. They are the chefs in the family, and are playing a big part in what shows up on the table. Best of all, they always want to learn more. This is truly exciting! I've also found that there are moms and dads who, because of hectic work schedules and the time constraints that go along with raising a family, have sadly never found the time to learn to cook. Therefore, they don't experience the joys that come with cooking together. I believe this has led to a lost connection between food and family. Well, EMERIL'S THERE'S A CHEF IN MY FAMILY! was written with you folks in mind. We'd like to encourage and help everyone believe that, yes, you *can* cook, and by helping you become comfortable and capable in the kitchen we hope to give you the satisfaction that comes from knowing that you are cooking good food and also providing your family with the opportunity to spend time together each day, no matter what your schedules.

Good food is at the heart of every cookbook, so we've chosen recipes that are tasty and nutritional, and that take you from breakfast to bedtime. They are guaranteed to kick your taste buds up a few notches! Having a good time is also at the heart of cooking, so we've chosen recipes that are fun to make as well as educational. Now you kids—don't get nervous about that last word. There are no tests involved, except seeing how fast your family gobbles up their food! But back to the educational part—we know from EMERIL'S THERE'S A CHEF IN MY SOUP! that cooking not only teaches us about food but also reinforces the skills involved in math, reading and following directions, using tools, and, most importantly, working well as part of a team. By cooking together, you will be strengthening all these skills.

On one last note: It has been a true blessing in my life to have kids come up to me and tell me I've left a mark in their lives—the same way other kids are influenced by firefighters, artists, athletes, or teachers. So if kids want to cook, I say encourage them, because I can tell you that cooking is an immensely satisfying profession as well as a wonderful hobby and a great skill to share with others. And hey—once you've mastered the basics, it's easy to keep building on your skills. When you're lucky enough to enjoy yourself in the kitchen, your family will always look forward to meals, and you'll always have that special time together.

HAPPY COOKING!

Chef Emeril

A GOOD COOK IS A SAFE COOK!

HEY, cooking is a lot of fun! I love everything about working in the kitchen—how the food looks, feels, and smells, and of course how it tastes when you're all done. But it's really important to remember that cooking is serious stuff. If you don't pay attention in the kitchen, you can get hurt very easily—and I want to be sure that doesn't happen. So before we get started, let's go over some ways to be safe in the kitchen.

ASK FOR HELP!

- Remember *always* to ask permission from your mom or dad or any adult in charge before you begin cooking.

- Never cook by yourself. It's always a good idea to have an adult nearby, especially when using sharp knives or graters, electrical appliances, hot burners, and the oven.

- You can do a lot of things yourself if you're careful, but ask for help when you need it—like lifting heavy pots. Being smart in the kitchen is important!

- You have to dress right for the kitchen—not to look good but to be safe and comfortable. Cooking clothes should be roomy but not too loose. Loose clothing can get caught on equipment, and you always have to be especially careful around an open flame. Long sleeves should be rolled up tight so they don't get in the way.

- Loose, long hair is a big no-no! If you have long hair, tie it back so it doesn't get in your way or into the food.

- Most jewelry isn't safe in the kitchen. Don't wear anything that dangles. If you wear a watch, be sure it's waterproof.

BE PREPARED!

- Always review the recipe you will be preparing before you begin. Make sure you have all the ingredients you need, and that all the tools and equipment are ready. Believe it or not, I still do this.

- If you don't understand how to do something, ask an adult to explain it to you before you begin cooking.

- I like to measure out all my ingredients before I start. I cut, chop, mince, and mix ahead when I can, too. It makes cooking a breeze.

● Cleanliness is very important in the kitchen. I know I sound like a grown-up but it's really true. You want the food you serve to be healthy and safe.

● Make sure you wash your hands well both before and after handling raw foods such as meat, poultry, eggs, and seafood. These items can sometimes contain harmful germs such as salmonella that can make you very sick. This can be prevented if you wash your hands and any tools that touched raw ingredients (knives, cutting boards, etc.) very well with warm to hot water and soap (preferably antibacterial), both before and after handling such ingredients.

● Here's a big secret we professional chefs have that I'll let you in on: It's a smart idea to clean up as you go along. That way, any tools that you need again will be clean and ready for you, and you'll have plenty of room on your counter to work. Best of all, you won't end up with a mountain of dirty dishes just when you want to be sitting down to enjoy your yummy creation.

● Never put knives or other sharp objects in sinks filled with water and other utensils—you can cut yourself when you reach into the water. It also damages the blades. It's best when working with knives to wash them well with soap and water as soon as you're finished with them.

● Cutting boards should always be washed with soap and warm water after each use. When you're using them to prepare raw meat or poultry, you have to be even more careful than usual! Unclean cutting boards can pass germs along to other foods. When in doubt wash, wash, wash.

STAY COOL WHEN COOKING WITH FIRE!

● It's really important to have an adult close by whenever you're cooking on the stove or in the oven, and they should be around from start to finish, when you turn the appliance off. Don't ever use the stove—or the oven—when you're home alone!

● Be extra careful of hot surfaces when cooking. It's easy to tell when a stovetop with a gas (open) flame is on; it's less obvious on stoves with electric or radiant burners, which are just as hot. Check your stovetop or oven controls carefully before you get to work.

● Pot holders and oven mitts rule in the kitchen! If you're not sure if something is hot, use pot holders or mitts just to be on the safe side. And hey—it's really important that pot holders and oven mitts are dry when you use them. If they're wet, the heat will go right through them and burn you faster than you can say, "Bam!"

● Never, ever leave food unattended while it's cooking!

● Always remember that the outside surface of the oven also gets hot when the oven is on, so don't lean against it when it's on.

- When cooking on top of the stove, always remember to turn your long pot handles to the side or toward the center. But make sure they're not over an open flame. They shouldn't hang over the edge of the stove, either—someone might walk by and knock into them by accident.

- Keep as far away as possible from hot, bubbling liquids. The bubbles can pop and splatter, and that can really burn. It's also a good idea to use long-handled wooden spoons to stir hot things.

- When moving heavy pots filled with hot liquids or when lifting heavy roasting pans out of the oven, you need to be smart. If you're sure you can do it, use pot holders and be really careful. If you even think for a minute that the pot or pan is too heavy for you, don't try to do it yourself. Ask an adult to help you!

- Remember always to uncover a hot pot so that the side of the lid farthest away from you tilts up first. This way the steam will be as far away from you as possible. Steam burns can really hurt! The same thing goes for draining a pot that is full of hot liquid—always pour out, away from you, so that the liquid and steam do not burn your hands or your face.

- If you do happen to burn or cut yourself, or in case of a fire, call an adult **immediately**_!_

KNOW YOUR TOOLS AND BE PATIENT!

- Kitchen tools are just like any other tools—you have to know how to use them the right way. This is for your safety and also to help you take care of your tools. If you're not familiar with the right way to hold and use knives or other equipment, ask your mom or dad or the supervising adult to show you, or check out our techniques section (pages 14–25) for the right ways to use most kitchen equipment.

- When learning how to work in the kitchen, be patient. It's better to practice any technique slowly—particularly chopping, slicing, or mincing. That way you can be precise and safe. You will be surprised to see that with just a little practice, you'll become good at it in no time.

- Watch out using graters—they're as sharp as knives! It's real easy to scrape fingers and knuckles when you're not paying attention.

- You have to be really careful when using electrical appliances such as the food processor, toaster, microwave oven, toaster oven, blenders, and mixers. These are powerful tools that should be used with caution. Here are some quick tips to follow at all times:

—Always be sure your hands are dry when you plug or unplug something.

—Never, ever put your hands or fingers inside any electrical appliance when it's on.

6

—Remember to pull your hair back and not wear dangling jewelry.

—Hey, make sure the lid on your blender is on tight—if it's not, your food will go all over the kitchen.

—Always turn your mixer *off* before scraping down the sides of the bowl or adding ingredients. If a spoon or spatula gets caught in the turning beaters, you'll ruin the mixer and maybe hurt yourself, too.

—When you turn the mixer back on after adding ingredients, start on the slowest speed. That way, your ingredients won't splash all over you.

—Food processors are great tools to use but they require special caution in order to be used safely. The blades are very sharp—be extra careful when removing or washing them. If you need to scrape down the sides of the bowl, do so with a long-handled rubber spatula. Never use your fingers for this! Also, it is especially important to always use the "feed tube" when adding ingredients to a processor that is already turned on. If you need to add something that won't fit through the feed tube, turn the processor off and remove the top. Do not under any circumstances attempt to turn the processor back on until the top is in place and the safety lock is engaged. Most newer food processor models already have safety features to protect you, but it never hurts to be extra careful!

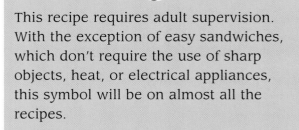

CAUTION

To help you stay safe, we've included little safety icons. You and your folks will know with one quick look how careful you'll need to be. Here's what they are and what they mean:

This recipe requires adult supervision. With the exception of easy sandwiches, which don't require the use of sharp objects, heat, or electrical appliances, this symbol will be on almost all the recipes.

This recipe requires the use of sharp objects such as knives or graters. You need an adult around to help, and you need to pay attention!

This recipe requires cooking either on the stovetop or in the oven. You have to be very, very careful and have an adult in the kitchen.

This recipe requires handling hot objects from either the stovetop or the oven. Be sure to use oven mitts or pot holders!

This recipe requires the use of electrical appliances.

This recipe requires the handling of raw meat, poultry, eggs, or seafood, which can carry germs. Wash your hands and tools with warm to hot water and soap before and after you touch these ingredients!

THE NUTS AND BOLTS

HERE ARE SOME of the tools you'll use most often in the kitchen.

1 | KNIVES

chef's knife   bread knife (serrated edge)   paring knife   butter knife

2 | CUTTING BOARDS

wood   plastic

3 | MIXING BOWLS

metal   glass   plastic

Note: Plastic or glass bowls should always be used when a recipe calls for a nonreactive bowl. Metal "reacts" with acidic foods such as vinegar and lemon juice, and this makes the food taste funny.

4 | SPOONS

wooden   metal   serving   slotted   skimmer

5 | COLANDERS

plastic   metal

6 | STRAINERS

coarse mesh   fine mesh   sieve   sifter

7 | MEASURING CUPS

glass   plastic   metal

8 | MEASURING SPOONS

plastic   metal

9 | WHISK

10 | SPATULAS AND TURNERS

rubber spatula   metal turner   plastic turner   wood turner

Note: Always use plastic or wood for nonstick pans so you don't damage their surfaces.

11 | TONGS

plastic   metal

12 | LADLE

13 | VEGETABLE PEELER

14 | VEGETABLE BRUSH

15 | GRATERS

box grater   single-sided

Note: A box grater has four sides: a single long slot for roughly slicing soft items such as cheese; a shredder side with large, widely spaced holes for shredding soft cheese, fruit, or vegetables; a coarse grating side for fruit and veggies and hard cheese; and a fine grating side for hard cheese, nuts, spices such as nutmeg, or for zesting citrus fruits (this will give you a very fine, almost powdery consistency). The single-sided grater usually has only coarse and fine grating capabilities.

16 | ZESTER

17 | KITCHEN SCISSORS OR SHEARS

18	POTATO MASHERS
19	GARLIC PRESS
20	APPLE CORER
21	PASTRY BRUSH
22	SKEWERS

metal   bamboo

Note: Always soak bamboo skewers in water for 30 minutes before using.

23	INSTANT-READ THERMOMETER
24	BULB BASTER
25	OVEN MITTS AND POT HOLDERS
26	ROLLING PIN
27	KITCHEN TIMER
28	COOKIE AND BISCUIT CUTTERS
29	MIXERS

handheld   standing electric

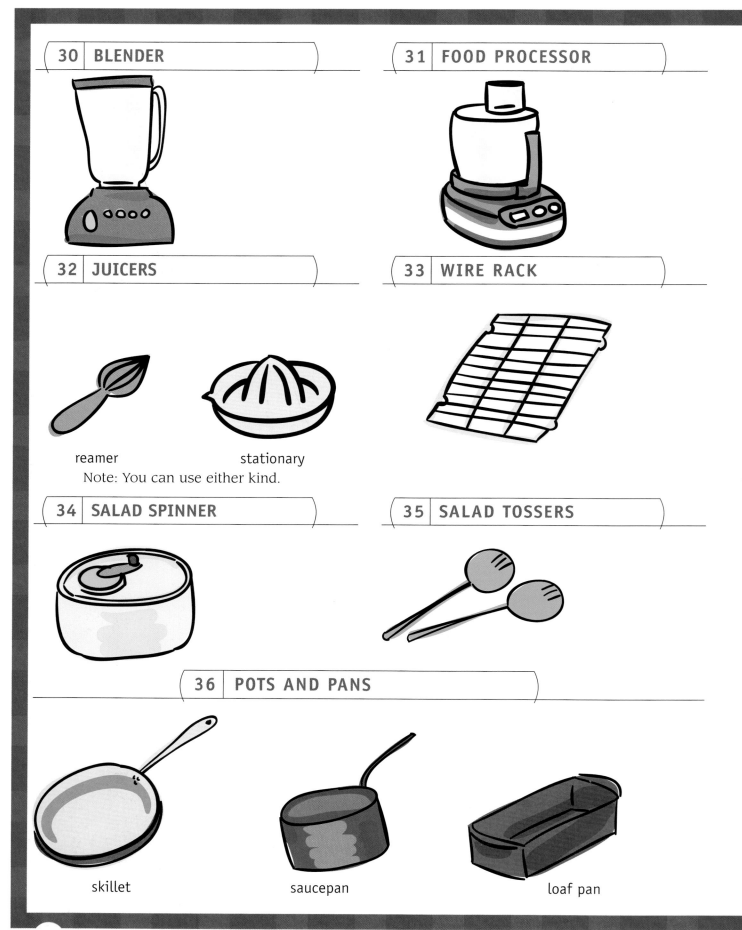

30	BLENDER		31	FOOD PROCESSOR

32	JUICERS		33	WIRE RACK

reamer   stationary

Note: You can use either kind.

34	SALAD SPINNER		35	SALAD TOSSERS

36	POTS AND PANS

skillet   saucepan   loaf pan

muffin pan

baking sheet

springform pan

baking dish

Dutch oven

cast-iron corn stick pan

37 | **FONDUE POT/CHAFING DISH**

38 | **COOKING AIDS**

paper muffin-tin liners

plastic wrap

parchment paper

aluminum foil

39 | **DOUBLE BOILER**

40 | **WAFFLE IRON**

GOOD THINGS TO KNOW

LET'S GET STARTED

WASHING

Fresh veggies and fruits should always be rinsed well under cold running water and then patted dry with paper towels before using. Berries and dried beans should be rinsed well and then "picked over," which simply means picking out and discarding any bad or blemished pieces. Some veggies, such as potatoes, need to be scrubbed well with a vegetable brush. Mushrooms need to be brushed with a soft-bristled brush in order to remove any loose dirt and, if washed, should not be allowed to soak in water.

Meat, poultry, and seafood should be washed before using, too. Simply rinse under cold water and then pat dry with paper towels before continuing.

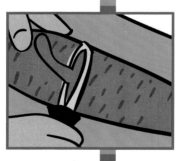

PEELING

Some fruits and veggies peel easily with a vegetable peeler. Place the food (such as a carrot, cucumber, potato, apple, or pear) on a cutting board and hold firmly with one hand. Using the other hand, scrape the peeler down the length of the food. Keep turning as you go, so that you remove all of the peel.

Other foods, such as onions and garlic, are peeled differently. Use a sharp knife to cut a little off of both ends. Then use your fingers to peel away the dry, tough outer layers. For garlic, press down on it with the palm of your hand to loosen the skin. It will then peel off very easily.

CHOPPING

When chopping round foods like potatoes or carrots, the first thing you should do is cut off a small piece from one side so that it doesn't roll away while you're cutting it. Place this flat part down on the cutting board. Then, hold one side of the food firmly with one hand and cut the food to the shape or size desired. The more you chop, the smaller the pieces will get.

When it comes to chopping, onions are in a league all their own! Once they're peeled, cut them in half lengthwise and place them flat side down on the cutting board. Then, while holding the root end with your

CUBED   ROUGHLY CHOPPED   FINELY CHOPPED   MINCED

fingers, make many lengthwise cuts all the way down to the cutting board. Then turn your knife and cut across the lengthwise cuts. Pieces of onion will fall away on the cutting board. The closer your cuts are to one another, the smaller the pieces of onion will be!

Mincing garlic is easy! Separate the head of garlic into cloves. Peel as described on page 14, then use your chef's knife or a paring knife to cut the cloves lengthwise and then crosswise into small pieces. (Another way to do this is with a garlic press, which is really easy and safe—and fun! Just put the garlic into the press, close it, and press real hard. Little pieces of garlic—just the right size—will come out of the holes!)

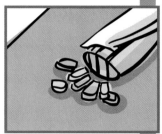

Fresh herbs can be chopped, too. Remove the leaves from any tough, woody stalks and chop with a chef's knife. Chives are easily chopped this way, or can be "snipped" using kitchen shears. Simply hold the bunch of chives in one hand and cut into small pieces with the scissors held in your other hand.

GRATING

When grating hard foods, like carrots or potatoes, hold the grater with one hand and the piece of food firmly in the other. Rub the end of the veggie downward over the holes, back and forth over a large mixing bowl or piece of waxed paper, and the grated pieces will fall through the holes. Be very careful not to grate your fingers—that hurts! Soft foods, such as cheese, are really easy to grate!

CORING APPLES

- **With an apple corer:** Hold the apple firmly on your cutting board. Center the apple corer over the core and press down firmly until you feel the corer hit the cutting board. Twist and pull corer out of the apple, and the core should come right out.

- **With a paring knife:** Cut the apple in half. Cut each half in half again. Place the apple on the cutting board and cut the core away from the apple.

- **With a melon baller:** This is the easiest way to core an apple! Cut an apple in half. Place the apple half on the cutting board, core side up. Hold the melon baller in your other hand and center it over the core of the apple. Press down into the apple and twist. A round piece of apple core should come right out.

HULLING STRAWBERRIES

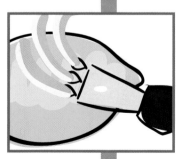

Place the strawberry on the cutting board and hold the pointed side with one hand. Using a paring knife, cut across the top to remove the stem.

FRUITS WITH PITS (SUCH AS PEACHES, NECTARINES, CHERRIES, PLUMS)

To remove the pit, simply cut the fruit in half along the indentation, then twist the two halves apart.

ZESTING

You can "zest" any citrus fruit (oranges, lemons, limes, or grapefruits). Using a "zester," it's really easy. Simply pull the zester down the side of a piece of fruit, pressing at the same time so that the zester removes tiny strips of the outermost

layer of peel. If you don't have a zester, a fine grater works too. Over a bowl or a piece of waxed paper, rub the side of the fruit along the grater while lightly pressing down. The small pieces of zest will fall through the grater. Be sure you get only the colored part of the peel: The white part is bitter!

JUICING ORANGES, LEMONS, LIMES, OR GRAPEFRUIT

Citrus fruits may be juiced in several ways. The easiest way is to cut the fruit in half crosswise, and then, while holding the fruit halves over a bowl to catch the juice, use your hands to squeeze the juice from the fruit. If you own a "reamer," simply hold one fruit half in one hand and insert the reamer into the fruit with the other hand while turning and pushing the reamer to extract the juice. Some folks have stationary juicers that are really a combination of a reamer and a shallow bowl or plate. These are easy to use—simply press the cut side of an orange, lemon, lime, or grapefruit down onto the cone-shaped reamer portion of the dish and twist with a continual downward pushing motion. The bowl portion of the juicer will collect the juice as you turn the fruit. Of course, if you have an electric juicer you can use that as well, but please be sure to follow the manufacturer's safety instructions and watch those fingers!

TRIMMING MEAT

It's a good idea to trim the excess fat off of meat before cooking. Simply use a very sharp knife and follow the line between the meat and the fat. If a little fat is left, that's okay.

PEELING AND DEVEINING SHRIMP

Shrimp should be deheaded, peeled, and deveined before using them for most recipes in this book. If you've never done this before, don't worry—it's easy! Hold the tail of one shrimp between the thumb and forefinger of one hand while grasping the head with the thumb and forefinger of the other hand. Pinch lightly where the head attaches to the tail while pulling it away from the tail, and the head should come right off. The thin outer shell, or peel, is easily removed by grasping one section at a time near where the legs are attached and peeling in a circular motion up and over the tail of the shrimp. The entire peel will usually come off in two or three motions. Once the peel is gone, run the tip of a sharp paring knife down the upper length of the tail of the shrimp, where you will sometimes see a dark vein. Remove the vein with your fingers or by running the shrimp under cold water. If a recipe instructs you to "butterfly" shrimp, that simply means making a deeper cut down the back of the shrimp so that the flesh opens up to resemble a butterfly.

CRACKING AND SEPARATING EGGS

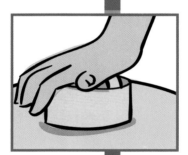

To crack an egg, hold it firmly in one hand while you hit the middle part (not too hard!) against the rim of a bowl. Then take both hands and grasp the cracked edges and pull apart. It's always a good idea to crack an egg into a separate bowl before adding it to a recipe so that you can see if any bits of shell fell into the egg. (If so, remove them before adding the egg to the recipe!) Sometimes a recipe will call for just egg yolks or egg whites. To separate eggs and use either the yolk or white only, crack the egg lightly and pull the halves apart, carefully letting the white drip into a cup. Keep the yolk in the eggshell. Gently move the yolk from one eggshell half to the other, letting the white drip into the cup until only the yolk is left in the shell. Be careful not to break the yolk so that it bleeds into the egg white.

CUTTING DOUGH WITH COOKIE CUTTERS

When cutting shapes out of rolled-out dough with cookie cutters, make sure to press down firmly to get a clean cut. And hey—if you don't happen to own any cookie cutters, don't worry! You can also use the rim of a sturdy glass or bowl. Measure the diameter of what you want to use to make sure it's the correct size, and then place the glass or bowl upside down onto the dough and press firmly, just as you would with a cookie cutter. Depending on the rim, this can make a clean cut. If not, use the tip of a sharp knife and trace the outer edge of the glass or bowl. Remove the glass or bowl and repeat to form the remaining cuts.

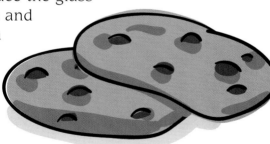

CUTTING CHICKENS

If a recipe calls for a whole chicken cut into pieces, please don't try to cut one up yourself. This is really hard and very dangerous. Either have your parents do it for you or buy a cut-up chicken at the grocery store.

REMOVING SAUSAGE FROM CASING

Sometimes sausage comes stuffed in "casing," which keeps it together. To remove the sausage from the casing, use the point of a sharp knife to cut the tip off of one end of the sausage link and squeeze from the bottom up to force the meat mixture out.

HOW TO KNOW WHEN ENOUGH IS ENOUGH

MEASURING

It's best to use individual ¼-, ⅓-, ½-, and 1-cup measuring cups when you can—it's the easiest and most accurate way to measure things. When measuring dry ingredients such as flour, sugar, or rice, use a metal or plastic measuring cup like that shown at right. Dip the appropriate size measuring cup into the ingredient that is to be measured, then use the flat side of a knife or your hand to level off the top.

When measuring liquids, use glass or plastic measuring cups that you can see through. Fill until the liquid comes to the appropriate line on the cup, checking at eye level to make sure you've measured the correct amount.

Measuring spoons are easy to use. For dry foods, just dip the spoons into whatever you're measuring, then level off the top. For liquids, such as oil or vanilla extract, hold the spoon in one hand and pour with the other. Make sure to hold the spoon level, and always fill it all the way to the top!

DETERMINING CONTAINER CAPACITY

If you're not sure of the size of a saucepan, baking dish, or other container, simply use a measuring cup to fill it with water. Count the number of cups it takes to fill the container and then figure out its size by referring to the equivalents chart on page 25.

NOW WE'RE COOKING

MIXING

Just another term for combining things, usually with a "mixer," which has beaters instead of spoons. Lock the beaters into the mixer, lower the beaters into the mixing bowl, then turn the power on slowly. As the mixture becomes more blended, you can increase the speed.

BEATING

This means mixing things together quickly so that air is added to the mixture and it becomes smooth and creamy. Usually done with a mixer, you can also beat things with a spoon—it just takes a little elbow grease!

STIRRING
Use a spoon to stir in a circular motion until the ingredients are all blended.

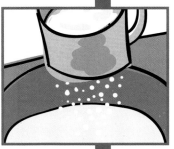

FOLDING
This is a way of mixing things together very gently so that they stay fluffy. Use a large plastic or rubber spatula and, instead of stirring, place it into the bowl and combine the ingredients with two or three up-and-over, or "folding," motions. Don't overmix!

SIFTING
This is done to make sure there are no lumps in dry foods like flour or sugar. Just hold the sifter over a bowl and shake from side to side (some sifters have knobs to turn or handles to squeeze).

CREAMING
This refers to beating butter and sugar together very well until it becomes light and "creamy."

SOFT OR STIFF PEAKS
These terms are used when beating things like heavy cream or egg whites. After you turn the mixer off and lift the beaters out of the bowl, if a little of the mixture comes up where the beaters were, forming soft mounds that stay up, those are soft peaks. When a recipe calls for stiff peaks, beat a little longer, until the mixture stands straight up and does not tip over when lifting out the beaters. Do not overbeat or the mixture will separate.

SCRAPING DOWN BOWL
This is done to make sure everything gets mixed evenly. Just hold the edge of the mixing bowl in one hand, then run a plastic or rubber spatula all the way around the inside of the bowl to "scrape down" the sides.

EGGS
Eggs come in different sizes. When using eggs for the recipes in this book, always use the ones labeled LARGE.

WORKING BUTTER INTO FLOUR
You can do this with a pastry blender, two forks or butter knives, or your fingers. The main thing is that the butter is rubbed into the flour so that only small pieces of butter are visible and the rest has been combined with the flour. When it's done, it will look like small crumbs.

SOFTENING BUTTER

If a recipe calls for butter to be softened, it means at room temperature—not straight from the refrigerator. If you forget to take the butter out to soften, try placing it in a microwave-proof bowl and microwave on high for 5 to 10 seconds. This works great.

ROLLING DOUGH

Place the dough on a lightly floured surface and sprinkle the top with flour. Using a rolling pin, roll while pressing down on the dough. Begin by rolling front to back, then switch directions and roll side to side. If the rolling pin sticks, sprinkle a little more flour. Continue rolling until the dough is the desired size and thickness.

BASTING

Basting is when you brush, spoon, or drizzle liquid—such as butter, meat drippings, or stock—over food as it cooks. Doing so helps to keep foods moist, adds flavor and color, and also helps form a crisp outer layer, especially for things like roast turkey or baked bread. You can baste by using a small brush, by spooning the liquid over cooking food with a large spoon, or by drizzling the liquid with the help of a bulb baster. If you don't have a brush made especially for basting, any small brush such as a pastry brush will work just fine.

BLANCHING

Blanching is done when foods such as vegetables and fruits are plunged into boiling water briefly, then quickly removed and usually transferred to cold water to stop the cooking process. This lightly cooks items that don't need lengthy cooking, and on such foods as tomatoes and peaches it can be used to loosen the skins so that they may be peeled easily.

GREASING A PAN

Greasing helps keep baked goods from sticking to the pan. It's easy to do this with your hands, but if you don't want to get your hands "dirty" then try using a paper towel to spread the shortening, oil, or butter. Just make sure you don't miss any spots!

Pans and other utensils also can be "greased" by spraying them with nonstick cooking spray. Simply shake the can well, hold it 6 to 12 inches away from the item, and spray until the item appears to be coated with a thin film of grease.

MEASURING THICKNESS OF DOUGH

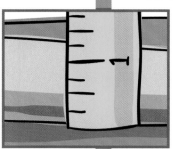

Until you have a lot of practice with this, it's a good idea to keep a ruler handy. This is an easy way to see if you've rolled your dough out to the correct thickness.

KNEADING DOUGH

Place the dough on a lightly floured surface. Use one hand to firmly press into one side of the dough. Pick up the other side of the dough with your other hand and fold it over, again pressing into the dough. Pick up the opposite edge of the dough and do the same. Repeat this process for as long as instructed in the individual recipe directions. The dough should become smooth and elastic. If the dough gets sticky, sprinkle with a bit more flour. You can also knead dough in an electric mixer if your mixer has a dough hook. Check manufacturer's instructions.

PROOFING YEAST

This is a way of making sure the yeast is working! Let it sit for about 5 minutes in a warm liquid. If it's working, you will see lots of foam and little bubbles rise to the surface.

SAUTÉING

This method of cooking comes from the French word meaning "to jump." It's a very accurate description because when you sauté, you quickly fry food in a small amount of fat. It tends to make the food pop and crisp quickly, so be sure to stir the mixture often and to keep an eye on it.

MELTING CHOCOLATE IN A DOUBLE BOILER

Fill the bottom part of a double boiler with about 2 inches of water. Insert the top part of the double boiler and place the chocolate in it. Set on the stovetop and simmer on low heat, stirring occasionally until the chocolate is melted. If you don't have a double boiler, you can use a medium saucepan for the bottom part and a metal bowl large enough to sit on top of the saucepan without touching the water in the bottom.

TOASTING THINGS

Many recipes call for toasted things, such as nuts or coconut and sometimes bread crumbs or croutons. This is pretty easy to do—just make sure you keep a close eye on whatever you're toasting because some foods toast quicker than others! You'll need either a toaster oven for small amounts or an oven for larger amounts, as well as a baking sheet large enough to hold whatever you're toasting in one even layer.

Make sure the oven rack is in the center position and preheat the oven to 350°F. Spread the desired amount of item to be toasted on a baking sheet and make sure it is spread evenly in one single layer. Whole nuts are best for toasting, though halves are okay, too. If the pieces are too small, this timing will be wrong and the nuts can easily burn. You can also chop after toasting if needed. Bake in the oven until just golden and very fragrant, 5 minutes for coconut and 8 to 10 minutes for most nuts. Using oven mitts or pot holders, carefully remove the baking sheet from the oven and transfer to a wire rack to cool. Use as desired or store in an airtight container, preferably in a cool location. Nuts will keep for up to 2 weeks after toasting. Coconut usually gets less crispy after a day or two.

IS IT DONE YET?

TESTING THE HEAT OF A PAN
You can test the heat of a pan by dropping a teaspoon of water in it. The pan is hot enough to cook in when the water "dances" into drops across the bottom.

TESTING WITH TOOTHPICKS
This is an easy trick! Insert a toothpick into the center of a cake near the end of the cooking time—if it comes out clean when you pull it out, the cake is done. If you can see gooey stuff or bits of crumbs sticking to it, then it needs a bit more cooking time.

THERMOMETER USAGE

Some recipes in this book suggest using an instant-read thermometer when things need to be at a certain temperature. Though this is not always necessary, a thermometer does help you make sure that things are cooked enough. Thermometers also help when cooking with yeast, because you usually need to add warm water or other liquid to it in order for it to start working. A thermometer will tell you if the liquid is too hot or too cold. (If you use a thermometer, make sure that it is inserted far enough into whatever you're testing so that you get a true temperature.)

FORK-TENDER
When you insert a fork into something and it goes in easily, then it is said to be fork-tender.

MEAT DONENESS

Because some meat may contain germs that can make you sick, it's a good idea to cook your meat until it's no longer pink inside. This is called being "cooked through." Even better, if you have an instant-read thermometer, simply insert the tip into the meat (there is usually a mark on the thermometer that shows how far it should be inserted), wait a few seconds until the temperature stops rising, and then read the number. For beef, medium well to well done is 150° to 165°F. For chicken, turkey, or pork, always cook to at least 160°F.

When testing for doneness on meat such as roast chicken and turkey, it is important that you place the thermometer in the deepest part of the joint between the leg and thigh, and equally important that the tip of the thermometer is not touching a bone. Have an adult help you master this technique!

COOKING WITH EGGS

When a recipe instructs you to cook eggs until they are "set," this means that the egg mixture should no longer be liquid or runny and should be firm when moved slightly.

KICK UP THE FLAVOR!

DRIED VS. FRESH HERBS

Most of the recipes in this book call for dried herbs, since this is what most folks have at home. It's really easy to kick them up a notch by rubbing them between your fingers before adding them to the recipe. They will release more flavor this way! And hey, if your mom or dad has an herb garden and you have access to fresh herbs, feel free to use them in recipes. Just take the leaves off of the stems and chop into small pieces with a knife. Remember, though, that if you want to use fresh herbs, you'll have to use about 3 times the dry amount called for in the recipe to get the same amount of flavor.

PEPPER

When a recipe calls for ground black pepper, the kind you buy in spice jars or tins is just fine. However, if you have a pepper mill at home, there's nothing like the flavor of fresh-ground pepper.

White pepper is a less pungent form of pepper that has a slightly different, milder flavor. It is most often used in light-colored dishes or those made with mild-flavored foods. If you don't have white pepper at home, simply substitute an equal amount of black pepper.

SALT

Kosher salt is an additive-free, coarse-grained salt. Some cooks prefer kosher salt's unique texture and flavor for specific uses. If you cannot find kosher salt in your grocery store, you can substitute sea salt or regular table salt. If you choose to substitute table salt, use only about half the amount called for.

BABY BAM | DIRECTIONS

YIELD: About 3/4 cup

INGREDIENTS

3 tablespoons paprika

2 tablespoons salt

2 tablespoons dried parsley

2 teaspoons onion powder

2 teaspoons garlic powder

1 teaspoon ground black pepper

1 teaspoon dried oregano

1 teaspoon dried basil

1 teaspoon dried thyme

1/2 teaspoon celery salt

TOOLS

Measuring spoons • small mixing bowl • wooden spoon • airtight container

Here's something to season your food the way adults do with Emeril's Original Essence. Give food another dimension by sprinkling Baby Bam into everything, from soups and sauces to pizza and hamburger patties. You fearless bammers out there can kick this up a notch by adding cayenne (I'd start with about 1/4 teaspoon, and then take it from there). Place all the ingredients in a small mixing bowl and stir well to combine, using a wooden spoon. Then store in an airtight container for up to 3 months.

MEASUREMENT EQUIVALENTS

3 teaspoons = 1 tablespoon

4 tablespoons = 1/4 cup

1 cup = 1/2 pint = 8 ounces

2 cups = 1 pint = 16 ounces

2 pints = 1 quart = 32 ounces

4 quarts = 1 gallon = 128 ounces

1 stick butter = 8 tablespoons = 1/4 pound = 1/2 cup

Beautiful
Beginnings

CHAPTER 1

IT'S-A-GOOD-MORNING MUFFINS

YIELD: 1 dozen muffins

INGREDIENTS

2 teaspoons unsalted butter

2 cups all-purpose flour

1 cup sugar

2 teaspoons baking soda

2 teaspoons ground cinnamon

$\frac{1}{2}$ teaspoon salt

1 cup grated carrots

1 cup grated parsnips

$\frac{1}{4}$ cup golden raisins

$\frac{1}{4}$ cup dark raisins

$\frac{1}{2}$ cup chopped pecans

$\frac{1}{2}$ cup shredded coconut

1 Granny Smith apple, peeled, cored
   and chopped

2 large eggs

1 cup vegetable oil

2 teaspoons vanilla extract

TOOLS

Muffin pan • muffin cups (optional) •
sifter • measuring cups and spoons •
vegetable peeler • box grater • 2
medium mixing bowls • wooden
spoon • whisk • oven mitts or pot
holders • wire rack

It's always a good morning when muffins are on
your family's breakfast table. But with these
muffins—oh yeah, baby! Not only are they super
delicious, but they're loaded with lots of good-for-
you things: carrots, parsnips, apples, pecans, and
raisins. Just try them! I bet a dozen muffins won't last
till lunchtime in your house! If you do have extras, they
make for great snacks and lunchbox treats.

1. Position rack in center of oven and preheat the oven to 350°F. If not using muffin cups then grease the wells of the muffin pan with the butter and set aside.

STEP 5

2. Sift the flour, sugar, baking soda, cinnamon, and salt into a mixing bowl. Stir in the carrots, parsnips, raisins, pecans, coconut, and apple.

3. In another bowl, combine the eggs, vegetable oil, and vanilla extract and whisk until smooth.

4. Add the wet mixture to the flour mixture and stir until the batter is just blended.

5. Spoon equal amounts of the batter into the wells.

6. Bake until the muffins spring back to the touch and are golden brown, about 35 minutes.

7. Using oven mitts or pot holders, carefully remove the muffins from the oven and transfer to a wire rack to cool for 5 minutes.

8. Remove the muffins from the muffin pan and set aside to cool completely.

TOTALLY-FROM-SCRATCH BISCUITS

YIELD: Eight 3-inch biscuits

INGREDIENTS

1¼ cups self-rising flour

¾ cup cake flour

1 tablespoon sugar

¾ teaspoon baking powder

½ teaspoon salt

⅛ teaspoon baking soda

4 tablespoons (½ stick) cold unsalted butter, plus 2 tablespoons melted butter

1¼ cups heavy cream

¼ cup all-purpose flour

TOOLS

Measuring cups and spoons • medium mixing bowl • sifter • pastry cutter (optional) • rubber spatula (optional) • 3-inch cookie cutter • baking sheet • small saucepan • pastry brush • oven mitts or pot holders

My friends! These biscuits are truly the real deal! Made totally from scratch, these will make you stop and think next time you consider using store-bought biscuits. Cake flour makes them extra tender, and heavy cream makes them super moist and delicious. Remember to go easy when mixing the dough or your biscuits will be tough and chewy instead of light and airy.

1. Position rack in center of oven and preheat the oven to 475°F.

2. Sift the self-rising flour, cake flour, sugar, baking powder, salt, and baking soda into a medium mixing bowl.

3. Using your fingers or a pastry cutter, work the cold butter into the flour until there are no butter pieces larger than a pea.

4. Add the heavy cream to the flour mixture and, using your hands or a rubber spatula, stir just until the cream and flour come together to form a dough. Do not overmix!

5. Sprinkle some of the all-purpose flour on a flat surface and place the dough on top of the flour. Using your hands, press the dough into a ½-inch thick disk about 8 inches in diameter.

STEP 5

6. Using a 3-inch round cutter dipped in flour, cut the dough into circles. Be sure to press straight downward when cutting the dough—a twisting motion will prevent the dough from rising. If you don't have a cutter, see page 18 for help. You will need to re-form the scraps of dough in order to make 8 biscuits. Do this by gathering the scrap pieces together and pressing to re-form into a ½-inch thick disk, then cut as many additional biscuits as possible from the re-formed dough.

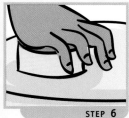

STEP 6

7. Place the biscuits on a small baking sheet and use a pastry brush to brush the tops with the melted butter.

8. Bake in the oven for 10 to 12 minutes, or until golden brown.

9. Using oven mitts or pot holders, remove the biscuits from the oven and allow to cool briefly and serve while still warm.

EGG-STRA SPECIAL OMELETS

YIELD: 1 serving

INGREDIENTS

3 large eggs

2 tablespoons heavy cream

1/8 teaspoon salt

Pinch of ground white pepper

1 tablespoon unsalted butter

3 tablespoons grated cheese, such as Cheddar or Swiss (optional)

TOOLS

Measuring spoons • blender • 8-inch nonstick skillet • heatproof rubber spatula • box grater (optional) • oven mitts or pot holders

Making omelets can be a bit tricky. But hey, if you follow the instructions below, you will end up with a light and fluffy omelet fit for a king! The blender is the key to super-fluffy eggs, so don't skip that step. Let everyone in the family design their own omelet by adding just what they like, such as steamed veggies, sautéed onions, chili, crumbled bacon, cubed ham, or—my personal favorite—cheese! Simply add any desired optional ingredients to the skillet along with the egg mixture.

1. Place the eggs, heavy cream, salt, and pepper in a blender and mix on high speed until very frothy, about 1 minute.

2. Heat a skillet over medium heat and, when hot, add the butter. When the butter has melted, swirl to coat.

3. Pour the egg mixture into the skillet.

4. Using a rubber spatula, stir continuously and scrape down sides to cook the mixture evenly.

5. After about 30 seconds, once the mixture resembles wet scrambled eggs, use the rubber spatula to smooth the eggs so that they are an even thickness throughout.

STEP 5

6. Cook until almost set (page 24), about 10 seconds longer, and use the rubber spatula to fold the omelet in half.

7. Carefully slide the omelet out of the skillet onto a plate.

8. Serve immediately.

STEP 6

If you want a cheesy omelet, sprinkle grated cheese over the omelet just before folding in half.

EMERIL'S FAVORITE FRIED EGG SANDWICH

YIELD: 1 serving

INGREDIENTS

1 tablespoon unsalted butter, softened

2 slices home-style white bread

1 slice ham

1 large egg

Pinch of salt

Pinch of ground black pepper

Optional ingredients of your choice

TOOLS

Butter knife • 12-inch skillet • metal spatula • oven mitts or pot holders

This has been my favorite way to eat an egg sandwich since I was a kid. Make one of these for your mom or dad and make them happy, happy. With a slice of ham and everything cooked in the same skillet— BAM! It's easy and delicious—what more can you ask for?

1 Using a butter knife and ½ tablespoon of the butter, coat one side of each slice of bread.

2 Heat a skillet over medium heat and, when hot, add the bread slices, buttered side down, to one side of the skillet.

3 After 30 seconds, add the remaining ½ tablespoon of butter to the other side of the skillet and, when melted, add the ham and egg to the skillet.

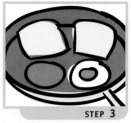

STEP 3

4 Season the egg with the salt and pepper. Using the edge of a spatula, pierce the egg yolk so that it runs. Allow to cook until the egg begins to firm and the ham browns, about 30 seconds.

5 Using the spatula, flip both the ham and the egg and continue to cook until both are done, about 30 seconds longer.

6 Using the spatula, stack the ham and egg on one unbuttered side of the toast, and top with the other slice, buttered side up.

STEP 6

7 Use the spatula to remove the sandwich from the skillet, transfer to a plate, and serve.

You can serve this sandwich with grated cheese, ketchup, or any extra toppings that your heart desires.

WAFFABLE WAFFLES

YIELD: Eight to ten 4-inch waffles

INGREDIENTS

2 cups all-purpose flour

2 teaspoons baking powder

1/2 teaspoon salt

4 large eggs, separated (page 18)

2 tablespoons sugar

2 cups whole milk

4 tablespoons (1/2 stick) unsalted
   butter, melted

1/2 teaspoon vanilla extract

Nonstick cooking spray

TOOLS

Small saucepan • waffle iron •
measuring cups and spoons • sifter •
3 medium mixing bowls • wooden
spoon • whisk • electric mixer •
rubber spatula • tongs or a fork •
oven mitts or pot holders

FRESH BERRY TOPPING

YIELD: 2 cups

INGREDIENTS

1 pound fresh strawberries,
   washed and hulled (page 16)

1/2 cup sugar

1/4 cup fresh-squeezed
   orange juice

1 teaspoon orange zest

TOOLS

Cutting board •
paring knife •
medium
mixing bowl •
measuring
cups and
spoons • zester
or box grater • juicer
(optional) • small
saucepan • wooden
spoon • oven mitts or
pot holders

What makes these waffles so waffable, you say? It's the beaten egg whites in the batter! The trick to light and airy waffles is to be quick and gentle when mixing the ingredients. And, when folding in the egg whites, remember that less is more! Don't forget—be gentle!

1 Make Fresh Berry Topping (page 39) and set aside.

2 Preheat a waffle iron according to the manufacturer's instructions.

3 Sift the flour, baking powder, and salt into a medium bowl. Set aside.

4 In a second bowl use a wooden spoon to beat together the egg yolks and sugar until sugar is completely dissolved and eggs have turned a pale yellow.

5 Add the milk, melted butter, and vanilla extract to the eggs and whisk to combine.

STEP 8

6 Add the flour mixture to the egg-milk mixture and whisk just until blended. Do not overmix.

7 In a third bowl, beat the egg whites with an electric mixer until soft peaks form (page 20), about 1 minute.

8 Using a rubber spatula, gently fold the egg whites into the waffle batter. Don't overmix!

STEP 9

9 Coat the waffle iron with nonstick cooking spray if required and pour enough batter in the iron to just cover waffle grid.

(continued)

> **CAUTION** Be careful not to touch the hot surface of the waffle iron or to close the lid on your fingers!

10 Close and cook as per manufacturer's instructions until golden brown, about 2 to 3 minutes. In checking for doneness, open the waffle iron carefully and watch out for steam. Do not open the waffle iron, though, for at least 1 minute. Repeat cooking with remaining batter. When each waffle is done, remove using either tongs or a fork. Don't forget to turn off the waffle iron when all the waffles are done.

11 Serve immediately with ¼ cup of the Fresh Berry Topping spooned over the top of each waffle.

FRESH BERRY TOPPING

This is a wonderfully simple strawberry topping that is super-easy to prepare. If you like, feel free to substitute part of the strawberries with other berries—blueberries, blackberries, or raspberries would all be great additions. Make it your own!

1 Slice strawberries into ¼-inch slices and place in a mixing bowl.

2 In a saucepan combine the sugar, orange juice, and orange zest and bring to a boil over medium heat. Stir with a wooden spoon to dissolve sugar.

3 Once syrup is at a rolling boil, remove from the heat and pour over the sliced strawberries. Let sit while cooking waffles.

> CAUTION
> Be really careful with boiling syrup—it's very sticky and can really burn if you get it on your skin.

4 Serve over waffles.

ONE-STOP BREAKFAST CASSEROLE

YIELD: 8 to 10 servings

INGREDIENTS

8 ounces breakfast sausage or bulk sausage, casing removed (page 18)

2 large shallots, minced (about $\frac{1}{3}$ cup)

1 tablespoon butter

12 to 16 $\frac{1}{2}$-inch-thick slices of day-old French bread (toast lightly if fresh)

6 ounces shredded cheese, such as Monterey Jack, Cheddar, or Swiss (1$\frac{1}{2}$ cups)

10 large eggs

2$\frac{1}{2}$ cups half-and-half

$\frac{1}{2}$ teaspoon salt

$\frac{1}{4}$ teaspoon ground white pepper

TOOLS

Cutting board • chef's knife • measuring cups and spoons • medium nonstick skillet • wooden spoon • 9-inch square baking dish • serrated bread knife • box grater • medium mixing bowl • whisk • plastic wrap • oven mitts or pot holders

One stop at this breakfast casserole will keep you happy till lunchtime. Because it can be assembled the night before, it's also just right to make for a brunch or when company is coming. In the morning, all you have to do is pop it in the oven to bake!

1. Heat a skillet over medium heat and, when hot, add the sausage. Cook until sausage begins to brown, breaking it into small pieces with a wooden spoon, about 4 minutes.

2. Add the shallots to the skillet and continue to cook until meat is golden brown and the shallots are soft, about 2 minutes longer.

3. Remove the skillet from heat and set aside.

4. Butter the baking dish and line the bottom with half of the bread slices.

5. Top the bread slices with half of the sausage-shallot mixture and half of the grated cheese. Make another layer with remaining bread, sausage, and cheese.

6. In a mixing bowl, combine the eggs, half-and-half, salt, and pepper and whisk to combine.

7. Pour the egg mixture evenly over the layered bread mixture. Cover with plastic wrap and refrigerate for at least 1 hour and up to overnight.

8. Remove the casserole from the refrigerator and allow to come to room temperature for about 20 minutes. Position rack in center of oven and preheat the oven to 325°F.

9. Remove the plastic wrap and bake the casserole, uncovered, until puffed and golden brown, about 1 hour.

10. Using oven mitts or pot holders, remove the casserole from the oven and let rest for 5 minutes before serving.

OOEY GOOEY BLUEBERRY "FRENCH TOAST"

YIELD: 10 to 12 servings

INGREDIENTS

1 tablespoon unsalted butter

14 slices home-style white bread, crusts discarded and bread cut into 1-inch cubes

2 (8-ounce) packages cold cream cheese, cut into 1-inch cubes

1 cup blueberries, picked over (page 14) and rinsed

10 large eggs

2 cups half-and-half

1/3 cup maple syrup

1/4 cup fresh-squeezed orange juice

TOOLS

Cutting board • serrated bread knife • 9 x 13-inch baking dish or casserole • chef's knife • juicer (optional) • measuring cups and spoons • large mixing bowl • whisk • aluminum foil • oven mitts or pot holders

BLUEBERRY SAUCE

YIELD: 3 cups

INGREDIENTS

1 1/2 cups sugar

1 1/2 cups water

1/2 cup fresh-squeezed orange juice

3 tablespoons cornstarch

1 1/2 teaspoons orange zest

1 1/2 cups blueberries, picked over (page 14) and rinsed

1 1/2 tablespoons unsalted butter

TOOLS Measuring cups and spoons • juicer (optional) • zester or box grater • small saucepan • wooden spoon • oven mitts or pot holders • large spoon or ladle

This dish is really a cross between French toast and bread pudding—two of my favorite things to eat any time of the day! It is rich and creamy and ooey and gooey and chock full of blueberries all at the same time. It's a great dish to make for a crowd and can be put together the night before and then baked in the morning, so that it's fresh and hot when you serve it. Don't skip the blueberry topping—it's the crowning glory!

1. Butter a baking dish with the tablespoon of butter.

2. Arrange half of the bread cubes on the bottom of the baking dish.

3. Top the bread cubes with the cream cheese cubes and blueberries and arrange the remaining bread cubes over the blueberries.

4. In a large bowl whisk together the eggs, half-and-half, syrup, and orange juice.

5. Pour the egg mixture evenly over the bread mixture. Cover with aluminum foil and refrigerate for at least 1 hour and up to overnight.

6. Remove the baking dish from the refrigerator and allow to come to room temperature for about 20 minutes. Position rack in center of oven and preheat the oven to 350°F.

7. Bake the "French toast" with foil cover for 30 minutes. Using oven mitts or pot holders, remove the baking dish from the oven, remove the foil, and return the dish to the oven until toast is golden brown and puffed, about 30 more minutes.

8. Using oven mitts or pot holders, remove the baking dish from the oven and allow to sit until slightly cooled, about 15 minutes.

9. Serve in bowls with blueberry sauce ladled over the top.

BLUEBERRY SAUCE

This is a truly delicious blueberry sauce that would be a wonderful addition to many other dishes—try it spooned over pancakes or waffles for a real treat. And hey—this can be made in advance and kept refrigerated for up to one week and then rewarmed just before serving.

1. In a small saucepan over medium-high heat, stir together the sugar, water, orange juice, cornstarch, and orange zest.

2. Cook, stirring occasionally, until thickened, about 5 minutes.

3. Stir in the blueberries and simmer the mixture, stirring occasionally, until the berries have burst, about 5 minutes.

4. Add the butter and stir until melted.

5. Remove from heat and spoon or ladle over warm Ooey Gooey Blueberry "French Toast."

DOUBLY DELICIOUS HOT CHOCOLATE WITH REAL WHIPPED CREAM

YIELD: 4 cups

INGREDIENTS

1/2 cup water

6 tablespoons Dutch-process cocoa powder

6 tablespoons sugar

3 cups whole milk

1/2 cup heavy cream

1/2 cup semisweet chocolate chips

1/2 teaspoon vanilla extract

TOOLS

Measuring cups and spoons • whisk • 2-quart saucepan • wooden spoon • ladle • oven mitts or pot holders

REAL WHIPPED CREAM

YIELD: About 1 cup

INGREDIENTS

1/2 cup heavy cream, well chilled

1 tablespoon confectioners' sugar

1/4 teaspoon vanilla extract

TOOLS

Medium metal or glass mixing bownd spoons • electric mixer (handheld or standing) • plastic wrap (optional) • oven mitts or pot holders

This is the perfect treat to make for your family on a cold, blustery morning. Well, come to think of it, this would be the perfect treat just about *any* morning in my house! With both cocoa powder and chocolate chips, it is a doubly delicious, doubly chocolaty hot chocolate. Your family will beg for more!

1 Place the water, cocoa, and sugar in a saucepan and whisk until smooth.

2 Place the saucepan over medium heat and cook for 1 minute, stirring constantly. Make sure your wooden spoon stirs the entire surface of the saucepan bottom—otherwise the cocoa will clump and your hot chocolate will not be smooth.

3 Add the milk, cream, chocolate chips, and vanilla extract to the saucepan, stirring constantly until the chocolate chips have melted and the hot chocolate is smooth and well blended, about 5 minutes.

4 Remove from the heat and ladle into mugs, garnishing each with ¼ cup of the Real Whipped Cream.

REAL WHIPPED CREAM

DIRECTIONS | CAUTION 👁 🔌

1 Place a mixing bowl and the beaters from your electric mixer in the freezer or refrigerator until well chilled, about 15 minutes.

2 Combine the heavy cream, confectioners' sugar, and vanilla extract in the mixing bowl.

3 With an electric mixer on low speed, begin beating the cream, gradually increasing the speed to high as cream thickens. (Do this slowly, or the cream will splatter all over!)

4 Beat until the cream forms soft peaks (page 20). Test to see if it is ready by turning off the mixer and lifting the beaters out of the cream—if the cream makes soft peaks that topple over slightly, then it's done. Be careful not to overwhip, or the cream will separate and begin to taste like butter.

5 Serve immediately or cover with plastic wrap and refrigerate for up to 2 hours.

STEP 4

The Bread Box

CHAPTER 2

NEVER-ENOUGH DINNER ROLLS

YIELD: 12 giant dinner rolls

INGREDIENTS

1¼ cups whole milk

¾ cup plus ½ teaspoon sugar

½ cup (1 stick) plus 2 teaspoons unsalted butter

3 tablespoons nonfat dry milk

1 teaspoon salt

1 (¼ ounce) packet active dry yeast

¼ cup warm water (110°F on an instant-read thermometer)

2 eggs, lightly beaten

4½ cups all-purpose flour

TOOLS

Measuring cups and spoons • small saucepan • wooden spoon • instant-read thermometer • 2 large mixing bowls • wax paper or plastic wrap • small bowl • rolling pin • cutting board • chef's knife • muffin pan • pastry brush • oven mitts or pot holders • wire rack

Because these rolls are so big and delicious, there never seem to be enough. Serve these to your family and you're sure to be a hit. I bet you'll all scramble to get the last one! These take some time, but if you start them just after lunch, I guarantee that you will have fresh, hot rolls just in time for dinner.

1 In a small saucepan over medium heat, combine the milk, ¾ cup of the sugar, 4 tablespoons (½ stick) of the butter, the dry milk, and the salt and cook, stirring frequently, until the butter is melted and the sugar has dissolved, about 2 to 3 minutes. Remove from the heat and set aside to cool to lukewarm before proceeding.

2 In a large mixing bowl, dissolve the yeast and remaining ½ teaspoon of sugar in the warm water. Set aside until foamy, about 10 minutes.

3 Add the milk mixture to the yeast mixture and stir to combine.

4 Add the eggs and stir to combine.

5 Stirring with a wooden spoon, add the flour to the egg and yeast mixture 1 cup at a time. The dough will be quite stiff and somewhat sticky. If the dough gets too stiff to stir with a spoon, use your hands to mix, but wash them first!

6 Lightly grease the inside of a large bowl with 1 teaspoon of the remaining butter. Transfer the dough to the bowl and turn the dough in the bowl to coat. Lightly grease a piece of wax paper or plastic wrap with another teaspoon of the butter and use it to cover the bowl, greased side down. Set aside in a warm place until dough has doubled in size, at least 3 hours.

7 Melt the remaining 4 tablespoons of butter and transfer to a small bowl to cool.

8 Turn the dough out onto a lightly floured surface and knead until smooth and elastic, about 2 to 3 minutes (page 22).

STEP 10

9 Using a lightly floured rolling pin, roll the dough to a thickness of ½ inch.

10 Using a sharp knife, cut the dough into 36 equal pieces. Tuck the cut edges of each piece under so as to form a smooth round ball of dough.

11 Place three balls of dough side by side into each well of a muffin pan. Using a pastry brush, lightly brush the top of each roll with some of the melted butter. Cover with plastic wrap and set aside in a warm, draft-free area until dough has doubled in size, about 1 hour.

STEP 11

12 Position rack in center of oven and preheat the oven to 350°F.

13 Remove the plastic wrap and bake the dinner rolls until golden brown and puffed, about 18 to 20 minutes.

14 Using oven mitts or pot holders, remove the muffin pan from the oven and let cool on a wire rack for a few minutes before serving.

STEP 11

YES-YOU-CAN BAGELS

YIELD: 12 bagels

INGREDIENTS

2 cups warm water (110°F on an
   instant-read thermometer)

4 tablespoons sugar

2 (1/4-ounce) packets active dry yeast

5 to 6 cups all-purpose flour

2 teaspoons salt

2 teaspoons vegetable oil

2 tablespoons yellow
   cornmeal

1 large egg yolk beaten
   with 1 tablespoon
   water

OPTIONAL TOPPINGS

1/2 cup lightly sautéed
   minced yellow onions
   (about 2 teaspoons per
   bagel)

2 tablespoons poppyseeds (about 1/2
   teaspoon per bagel)

2 tablespoons sesame seeds (about 1/2
   teaspoon per bagel)

1 tablespoon kosher salt (about 1/4
   teaspoon per bagel)

TOOLS

2 large mixing bowls • standing
electric mixer fitted with a dough
hook (optional) • measuring cups and
spoons • instant-read thermometer •
wooden spoon • kitchen towel or
plastic wrap • pastry cutter or knife
for cutting dough • large baking
sheet • large heavy pot preferably at
least 10 to 12 inches in diameter •
slotted spoon or skimmer • paper
towels • small bowl • fork • pastry
brush • oven mitts or pot
holders • wire rack

Don't let the number of steps in this recipe fool you—
bagels are very easy to make at home. Just be sure to
follow the instructions on kneading and resting the
dough, and you will end up with 12 big, super-light
bagels! If the dough is too thick for you to
mix and knead by hand, a standing
electric mixer fitted with a dough
hook will help you out. You'll
never go back to store-bought
bagels again!

DIRECTIONS   CAUTION

1 In a large bowl, combine the water, 3 tablespoons of the sugar, and
   yeast. Stir and let stand until foamy, about 5 minutes.

2 Gradually add 4 cups of the flour and the salt to the mixture and stir
   well with a wooden spoon just until the mixture comes together.

3 Add 1 to 1½ cups of the remaining flour, ½ cup at a time, until a stiff dough is formed. If dough is too stiff to mix with a spoon, transfer it to a standing electric mixer fitted with a dough hook and knead the dough.

4 Turn dough out onto a lightly floured surface and knead with your hands until smooth and no longer sticky, about 5 minutes (page 22). If dough seems sticky, add a bit of the remaining flour until it is no longer so. This should be a very stiff and heavy dough.

5 Lightly oil a large bowl with 1 teaspoon of the vegetable oil and place the dough in the bowl, turning to coat. Cover the bowl with a damp clean kitchen towel or plastic wrap and set aside to rise in a warm, draft-free area until dough has almost doubled in size, about 1 hour.

6 Remove the dough from the bowl and punch dough down with your fist.

STEP 6

7 Divide the dough into 12 equal pieces and form each piece of dough into a ball. Stick your finger through the middle of the dough to make a hole. Using your fingers, smooth the top and sides of the dough and pull the sides gently apart to enlarge the hole and make a circle about 3 to 3½ inches in diameter. Repeat with the remaining pieces of dough.

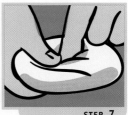

STEP 7

8 Place the bagels on a lightly floured surface, cover with a damp clean kitchen towel and set aside to rest in a warm, draft-free area until dough has risen but *not* doubled, about 15 to 20 minutes.

9 Position rack in center of oven and preheat the oven to 400°F. Lightly grease a baking sheet with the remaining teaspoon of vegetable oil and sprinkle lightly with the cornmeal.

10 In a large, heavy pot, bring 12 cups of water to a boil with the remaining tablespoon of sugar.

11 Carefully lower the bagels into the boiling water in batches, leaving enough room for them to expand as they cook (usually 3 or 4 per batch, depending on the size of your pot). Cook for 5 minutes, turning once midway through the cooking time using a slotted spoon.

12 Using a slotted spoon or skimmer, remove the boiled bagels and set aside to drain on paper towels.

STEP 12

13 Transfer bagels to the prepared baking sheet with the slotted spoon and brush each with the beaten egg mixture. Sprinkle with the optional toppings, if desired, and bake until golden brown and crusty, about 25 to 30 minutes.

14 With oven mitts or pot holders, remove the baking sheet from the oven and transfer the bagels to a wire rack to cool.

HOT-OUT-OF-THE-OVEN BREAD

YIELD: 2 loaves, serving 10 to 12 per loaf

INGREDIENTS

3 cups warm water (110°F on an instant-read thermometer)

2 tablespoons sugar

3 ($\frac{1}{4}$-ounce) packets active dry yeast

7 to $7\frac{1}{2}$ cups white bread flour

$\frac{1}{3}$ cup nonfat dry milk

4 tablespoons ($\frac{1}{2}$ stick) unsalted butter, at room temperature

1 tablespoon salt

2 teaspoons vegetable oil

TOOLS

Measuring cups and spoons • wooden spoon • instant-read thermometer • standing electric mixer fitted with a dough hook • large mixing bowl • kitchen towel or plastic wrap • cutting board • serrated knife • two 6 x 9-inch nonstick loaf pans • plastic wrap • baking sheet • oven mitts or pot holders • wire rack

Nothing smells better than bread baking in the oven, and nothing tastes better than bread hot out of the oven. You're going to love making this for your family. Keep in mind that this bread needs quite a bit of kneading, so a standing electric mixer works best. If you don't have one, don't worry! You can knead the bread by hand, but it will take some extra time and muscle!

1. In the bowl of a standing electric mixer fitted with a dough hook combine the water, sugar, and yeast and stir to combine. Set aside until the yeast mixture is foamy, about 5 to 10 minutes.

2. Add 7 cups of the bread flour, the dry milk, butter, and salt, and mix on low speed until dough comes together to form a ball, about 2 to 3 minutes. Turn the mixer off and poke the dough. If your finger comes away with some dough on it, it is still too wet, and you need to add some of the remaining flour in $\frac{1}{4}$-cup increments and continue to mix until the flour is incorporated and your finger remains dry when you poke the dough again.

3. Increase speed to medium and mix for 8 minutes, until the dough is smooth and elastic.

4. Using your fingers, lightly coat a mixing bowl with the vegetable oil.

STEP 6

5. Transfer the dough to the bowl and turn to coat. Cover the bowl with a damp clean kitchen towel or a piece of plastic wrap and set aside in a warm, draft-free area to rise until dough has doubled in size, about 1 to 1$\frac{1}{2}$ hours.

6. Punch down the dough with your fist and transfer to a cutting board. Using a sharp serrated knife, cut the dough into two equal portions.

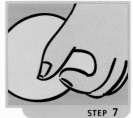
STEP 7

7. Use your hands to roll or tuck the outer edges of each dough portion underneath, so that the top of the dough is smooth and rounded. Place each ball of dough into a loaf pan and press it into the corners so that the dough is evenly distributed. Cover the pan with plastic wrap and set aside in a warm, draft-free area to rise until dough has doubled in size, about 30 to 45 minutes.

8. Position rack in center of oven and preheat the oven to 400°F.

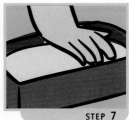
STEP 7

9. Place the two loaf pans on a baking sheet and bake in the middle of the oven until bread is golden brown and makes a hollow sound when tapped on the top, about 25 to 30 minutes.

10. Using oven mitts or pot holders, remove the baking sheet from the oven and remove the loaves from the pans. Transfer the loaves to a wire rack to cool, at least 20 to 30 minutes.

CAUTION | Always be sure the mixer is off before you add ingredients to the bowl or check the dough.

EVERYONE LOVES CORNBREAD

YIELD: One 10-inch round cornbread, or 12 pieces

INGREDIENTS

1/2 cup plus 2 teaspoons vegetable oil

2 large eggs

1 cup sour cream

1 cup canned creamed corn

1 1/2 cups cornmeal

2 tablespoons sugar

2 teaspoons baking powder

1/2 teaspoon salt

TOOLS

Measuring cups and spoons • 10-inch cast-iron skillet • 2 medium mixing bowls • whisk • can opener • wooden spoon • sifter • oven mitts or pot holders • toothpick

This cornbread is baked the real Southern way—in a preheated iron skillet that gives it a crispy outer crust and a soft, moist center. But don't panic if you don't have an iron skillet—just use another type of baking dish, and follow the same directions. I suggest making a double batch if your family loves cornbread as much as mine does!

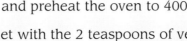
1. Position rack in center of oven and preheat the oven to 400°F.

2. Grease a 10-inch cast-iron skillet with the 2 teaspoons of vegetable oil and heat in the oven for 15 minutes.

3. Meanwhile, whisk the eggs in a medium bowl until frothy, about 1 minute. Add the remaining ½ cup of vegetable oil and the sour cream and whisk until combined.

4. Using a wooden spoon, stir the creamed corn into the egg mixture and set aside.

5. Sift the dry ingredients—the cornmeal, sugar, baking powder, and salt—into another medium bowl.

6. Stir the wet mixture into the dry mixture just until combined.

7. Using oven mitts or pot holders, remove the hot skillet from the oven. Carefully pour the cornbread batter into the skillet.

STEP 7

8. Using oven mitts or pot holders, return the skillet to the oven and bake the cornbread until it is a light golden brown and a toothpick inserted in the center comes out clean (page 23), about 25 minutes.

9. Using oven mitts or pot holders, remove the skillet from the oven and let cool briefly before serving. Serve warm with butter.

CAUTION Hey, watch it! You're handling a very hot and heavy pan. Make sure an adult is in the kitchen to help.

FOCACCIA, ANYONE?

YIELD: 1 large "loaf" of focaccia, about 12 inches by 17 inches

INGREDIENTS

7 tablespoons extra-virgin olive oil

3 (¼-ounce) packets active dry yeast

2 teaspoons brown sugar

2 cups warm water (110° on an instant-read thermometer)

6 cups white bread flour

1 teaspoon salt

1 tablespoon kosher salt

¼ cup chopped fresh basil

TOOLS

Large rimmed baking sheet, about 12 x 17 inches • measuring cups and spoons • standing electric mixer fitted with a dough hook • large mixing bowl • instant-read thermometer • kitchen towel or plastic wrap • oven mitts or pot holders • cutting board • chef's knife • wire rack

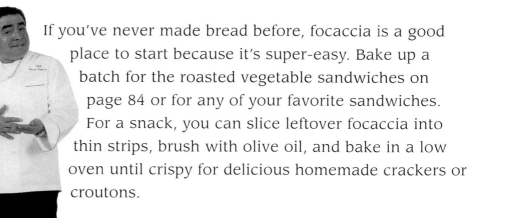

If you've never made bread before, focaccia is a good place to start because it's super-easy. Bake up a batch for the roasted vegetable sandwiches on page 84 or for any of your favorite sandwiches. For a snack, you can slice leftover focaccia into thin strips, brush with olive oil, and bake in a low oven until crispy for delicious homemade crackers or croutons.

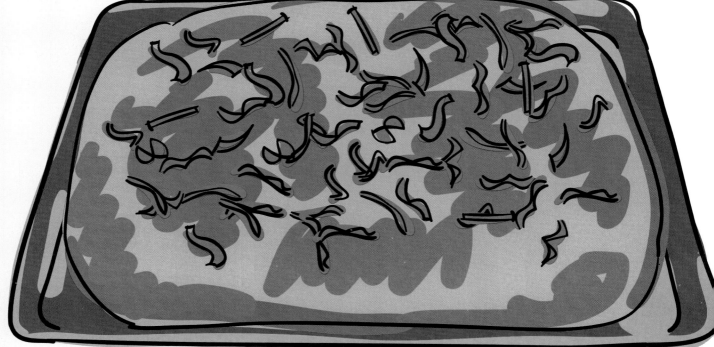

1. Lightly oil a baking sheet with 2 teaspoons of the olive oil.

2. In the bowl of a standing electric mixer fitted with a dough hook, combine the water, sugar, and yeast with 4 tablespoons of the remaining olive oil. Stir and let sit until foamy, about 5 minutes.

3. Add the flour and regular salt and mix on low speed until the dough comes together and forms a ball, about 2 to 3 minutes.

STEP 3

4. Increase speed to medium and mix for 7 to 8 minutes. If the dough is a little sticky, continue mixing and, with the mixer on low speed, add a bit more bread flour to form a smooth, elastic dough.

5. Coat a large mixing bowl with 1 teaspoon of the remaining olive oil. Transfer dough to the bowl and turn to coat evenly with the oil. Cover the bowl with a damp clean kitchen towel or plastic wrap and put in a warm, draft-free area to rise until dough has doubled in size, about 1½ hours.

6. Position rack in center of oven and preheat the oven to 450°F.

7. When the bread dough has doubled, punch the dough down with your fist and transfer to the greased baking sheet. Using your fingers, press the dough evenly to about ½-inch thickness.

STEP 7

8. Cover with plastic wrap, put in a warm, dry area, and let rise until doubled in size, about 30 minutes to 1 hour.

9. Remove the plastic wrap and, using your fingertips, press to form dimples in the dough at about 3-inch intervals. Sprinkle with the kosher salt and drizzle with the remaining 2 tablespoons of olive oil.

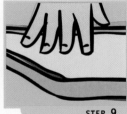
STEP 9

10. Bake until golden, about 25 to 30 minutes. (You may need to turn the baking sheet once during the cooking time to ensure even browning.)

11. Using oven mitts or pot holders, remove the baking sheet from the oven and transfer to a wire rack. Sprinkle the focaccia with the chopped basil and set aside to cool.

> **CAUTION** Always be sure to turn off the mixer before handling the dough.

TRY IT, YOU'LL LIKE IT ZUCCHINI BREAD

YIELD: 1 large loaf or 2 small loaves, serving 10 to 12

INGREDIENTS

1½ teaspoons unsalted butter

3 large eggs

¾ cup vegetable oil

2 teaspoons vanilla extract

1½ cups sugar

2½ cups grated zucchini or yellow squash

2½ cups all-purpose flour

1 teaspoon ground cinnamon

1 teaspoon baking soda

¾ teaspoon salt

¼ teaspoon baking powder

½ cup chopped pecans or walnuts (optional)

TOOLS

6 x 9-inch loaf pan • 1 large and 1 medium mixing bowl • whisk • measuring cups and spoons • box grater • sifter • rubber spatula • toothpick • oven mitts or pot holders • wire rack • cutting board • chef's knife

I bet many of you might be saying to yourselves, "Self, is he really making bread with *zucchini*?" The answer is YES! If you've never tried it before, this is going to make you look at zucchini in a whole new way. The "bread" is really more like a very moist spice cake. Bake some for after-school treats or lunch-box snacks!

1 Position rack in center of oven and preheat the oven to 350°F.

2 Grease a 6 by 9-inch loaf pan with the butter and set aside.

3 In a large bowl, whisk the eggs until yellow and frothy.

4 Add the vegetable oil, vanilla extract, and sugar and whisk to combine.

5 Add the zucchini and mix well.

6 Sift together the flour, cinnamon, baking soda, salt, and baking powder into a medium bowl.

7 Add the dry ingredients to the wet ingredients and, using a rubber spatula, mix just until blended, being careful not to overmix. Fold in the nuts, if desired.

8 Pour into the prepared loaf pan and bake until risen and golden brown, about 1½ hours. A toothpick inserted into the middle should come out clean (page 23).

9 Using oven mitts or pot holders, remove the loaf pan from the oven and let cool in the pan for 10 minutes. Turn the bread out onto a wire rack, setting it right side up, to cool completely before cutting.

> The bread may also be baked in two small loaf pans. Decrease the cooking time to about 1 hour.

Sensational Salads

CATCH A SHRIMP COCKTAIL

This is a true classic that everyone loves—and now you can make it at home for family parties or backyard barbecues! Just keep in mind that we used medium shrimp. If you use larger or smaller shrimp, you will need to adjust the cooking time, a little less for the small shrimp and a little more for the jumbo ones. Make the Cocktail Sauce mild or spice it up—you choose.

YIELD: 4 servings

INGREDIENTS

1 pound medium shrimp (about 30 per pound), deheaded but with peels still on (you can use fresh or thawed, frozen shrimp)

3 cups water

1 rib celery, cut into 1-inch pieces

3 sprigs fresh parsley

1 sprig fresh tarragon

1 sprig fresh thyme

1 bay leaf

Juice and rind of $1/2$ lemon

2 teaspoons white wine vinegar

2 teaspoons salt

$1/2$ teaspoon Baby Bam (page 25)

$1/4$ teaspoon whole black peppercorns

$1/4$ teaspoon coriander seeds

4 lemon wedges for garnish

TOOLS

Paring knife • $2^1/_2$- to 3-quart saucepan with lid • measuring cups and spoons • juicer (optional) • wooden spoon • strainer or colander • large bowl • oven mitts or pot holders

COCKTAIL SAUCE

YIELD: About 1 cup

INGREDIENTS

1 cup ketchup

1 tablespoon fresh lemon juice

1 teaspoon prepared horseradish

$1/2$ teaspoon Worcestershire sauce

$1/4$ teaspoon salt

$1/4$ teaspoon ground black pepper

TOOLS

Measuring cups and spoons • juicer (optional) • small mixing bowl • wooden spoon • plastic wrap

1. Peel the shrimp (page 17), leaving the tail segment on so you can have a little handle. Using a paring knife, make a shallow slit down the back of each shrimp and remove the black vein. Discard the black veins and set shrimp aside.

STEP 1

2. In a medium saucepan, combine the remaining ingredients (except lemon wedges for garnish) and bring to a boil over high heat.

3. Add the shrimp to the boiling water, stir, cover, and remove from the heat. Let stand for 8 to 10 minutes.

4. Strain the shrimp in a colander set in the sink and transfer the shrimp to a large bowl. Discard the cooking liquid and seasonings.

STEP 1

5. Refrigerate the shrimp until well chilled, about 1 hour. While the shrimp are chilling, make the Cocktail Sauce below.

6. When ready to serve, divide the shrimp among four small bowls and hang them on the rim of each bowl.

7. Spoon an equal amount of cocktail sauce into the bottom of each bowl. Garnish each bowl with a lemon wedge. Alternatively, you can arrange a layer of crushed ice in the bottoms of four bowls, put a small dish of cocktail sauce in the ice, and arrange the shrimp on the ice around the sauce.

STEP 6

COCKTAIL SAUCE

Though this sauce is pretty tasty as it is, for you heat lovers out there, kick things up a few notches by adding some hot sauce or even a bit more horseradish. Oh yeah, baby. Now we're talking!

DIRECTIONS

1. Combine all the ingredients in a mixing bowl and stir to blend. Cover with plastic wrap and chill in the refrigerator until ready to serve. (Sauce can be made in advance and will keep for up to 1 week in the refrigerator.)

MY KINDA SALAD

YIELD: 4 large salads or 6 to 8 side salads

INGREDIENTS

1 (8-inch) piece of French bread, crust trimmed, cut into $1/2$-inch cubes (about 3 cups)

1 teaspoon Baby Bam (page 25)

1 cup olive oil

$1 1/2$ teaspoons chopped garlic

2 tablespoons white wine vinegar

1 tablespoon Dijon mustard

1 tablespoon balsamic vinegar

1 teaspoon lemon zest

1 teaspoon sugar

$1/2$ teaspoon Emeril's Italian Essence or other dry Italian seasoning

$1/4$ teaspoon salt

$1/8$ teaspoon ground black pepper

1 head romaine lettuce, washed and dried, torn into bite-size pieces (about 10 cups)

$1/2$ cup grated Parmesan cheese

TOOLS

Baking sheet • parchment paper or aluminum foil • cutting board • chef's knife • serrated knife • measuring cups and spoons • 2 medium mixing bowls • blender • rubber spatula • oven mitts or pot holders • zester • whisk • large salad bowl • box grater

This salad was inspired by the classic Caesar salad, but I've added my own twists to make it my kind of salad. The flavors go well with lots of things, and I often make this at home for my family—try it as a side salad next to a big bowl of pasta, or change it into a main event by topping it with grilled chicken or shrimp. The crispy romaine lettuce has lots of places for the grated Parmesan cheese to hide, and the light, lemony dressing adds just the right tang! You've gotta love it!

1 Position rack in center of oven and preheat the oven to 350°F. Line a baking sheet with parchment paper or aluminum foil.

2 To make the croutons, put the bread cubes in a medium mixing bowl and season with the Baby Bam.

3 Combine ⅓ cup of the olive oil and 1 teaspoon of the garlic in a blender and process on high speed for 30 seconds.

CAUTION

> Be sure to put the top of the blender on tightly before turning it on—otherwise you'll have food all over the kitchen!

4 Add the olive oil mixture to the bread cubes and toss with a spatula to coat evenly.

5 Spread the bread cubes evenly on the lined baking sheet and bake until lightly browned, about 20 minutes.

6 Using oven mitts or pot holders, remove the baking sheet from the oven and set aside to cool.

7 To make the dressing, combine the white wine vinegar, mustard, balsamic vinegar, lemon zest, sugar, Italian Essence, salt, pepper, and remaining ½ teaspoon of garlic in a medium mixing bowl. Whisk to blend. Gradually add the remaining ⅔ cup of olive oil in a thin stream, whisking constantly until well blended and smooth.

8 To assemble the salad, put the lettuce in a large salad bowl and add the dressing and the Parmesan cheese. Toss to coat evenly. Divide the salad mixture evenly among 4 salad plates (or more if making smaller servings) and top with equal amounts of the croutons.

POWER-PACKED SPINACH SALAD

YIELD: 4 large salads or 6 to 8 side salads

INGREDIENTS

8 slices bacon

10 cups fresh spinach, rinsed, stemmed, and patted dry

2 cups white button mushrooms, wiped clean, trimmed, and sliced

1 cup thinly sliced red onion

2 medium tomatoes, cored and cut into wedges (optional)

2 hard-boiled eggs, peeled and thinly sliced (optional)

TOOLS

Small baking sheet • parchment paper • oven mitts or pot holders • cutting board • chef's knife • measuring cups and spoons • large mixing bowl • wooden spoon or two forks

DRESSING

YIELD: 1 cup

INGREDIENTS

$1/2$ cup honey

$1/4$ cup Dijon mustard

1 cup vegetable oil

2 tablespoons fresh lemon juice

$1/2$ teaspoon ground white pepper

$1/4$ teaspoon salt

TOOLS

Cutting board • chef's knife • measuring cups and spoons • medium mixing bowl • whisk • juicer (optional)

Spinach and bacon—talk about a classic combination. And it also happens to be packed with that good-for-you protein! To make things easy, you can cook the bacon in the oven—no splatters to clean up and you can be doing other things at the same time. Here's how I'd do it: While the bacon is cooking, make the salad and the dressing. This way, once the bacon is done and cooled, you're ready to go!

1. Position rack in center of oven and preheat the oven to 375°F.

2. Line a baking sheet with parchment paper and arrange the bacon strips on it. Bake until brown and crispy, about 20 to 25 minutes.

3. Using oven mitts or pot holders, remove the bacon from the oven and let cool, about 15 minutes. Crumble into bite-size pieces.

4. Combine the spinach, bacon, mushrooms, and onion in a large mixing bowl and toss.

5. Divide the spinach mixture among 4 large plates or 8 small plates (either 2-cup or 1-cup portions).

6. Garnish with tomato wedges and/or sliced hard-boiled eggs if desired. Drizzle with the dressing and serve.

DRESSING

DIRECTIONS

1. Combine the honey and mustard in a medium mixing bowl and whisk to blend.

2. Slowly add the oil in a steady stream, whisking until blended and smooth.

3. Add the lemon juice, white pepper, and salt and whisk to blend.

STEP 2

BEANS GALORE SALAD

YIELD: 2 quarts,
serving 10 to 12

INGREDIENTS

$1/2$ cup dried red kidney beans
soaked overnight or $1^1/2$ cups
canned, drained, and rinsed red
beans

$1/2$ cup dried black beans soaked
overnight or $1^1/2$ cups
canned, drained, and rinsed
black beans

$1/2$ cup dried cannellini, navy, or
Great Northern beans soaked
overnight or $1^1/2$ cups canned,
drained, and rinsed white beans

12 cups water

3 peeled whole garlic cloves, plus 1
teaspoon minced garlic

$1^1/2$ cups red wine vinegar

1 cup plus 2 tablespoons
sugar

$3/4$ cup vegetable oil

1 teaspoon salt

$1/2$ pound fresh wax
beans, ends
trimmed and
blanched until
crisp-tender (page
21)

$1/2$ pound fresh green
beans, ends trimmed
and blanched until
crisp-tender

$1/2$ medium red onion,
chopped (about $1/2$
cup)

TOOLS

4 medium saucepans • cutting
board • chef's knife • measuring cups
and spoons • oven mitts or pot
holders • colander • large glass or
other nonreactive bowl • plastic wrap
• medium glass or other nonreactive
bowl • wooden spoon • can opener
(optional)

Talk about a great salad to take on a picnic or
bring to a family reunion. Everyone loves this
sweet and tangy salad that has—believe it or
not—*five* different kinds of beans! If you make
it a day or two in advance, it will
taste even better. I'm telling you,
you're guaranteed to be a hit with
this one!

1 If using canned beans, go directly to the end of step 4.

2 If using dried, soaked beans, put the red beans, black beans, and cannellini in separate saucepans. Add four cups of water and one garlic clove to each pot.

3 Over high heat, bring each pot to a boil, reduce the heat to medium-low, and cook until the beans are just tender, about 30 to 45 minutes. *Note*: These cooking times will vary from one package of dried beans to another.

4 Using oven mitts or pot holders, carefully pour the liquid and the beans away from you into a colander set in the sink. Rinse with cool water, and then transfer the beans to a large nonreactive bowl and cover with plastic wrap. Refrigerate, stirring occasionally, until thoroughly chilled, at least 2 hours.

> **CAUTION**
> Be very careful of steam from boiling liquids—it can burn you! Always pour hot liquid away from you.

5 In a saucepan over high heat, combine the red wine vinegar, sugar, oil, salt, and the minced garlic. Cook until the sugar is dissolved, about 5 minutes. Transfer to a medium, nonreactive bowl, cover with plastic wrap, and refrigerate until thoroughly chilled, at least 2 hours.

6 Add the blanched wax beans, green beans, vinegar mixture, and onion to the beans in the large bowl and toss to mix thoroughly. Serve immediately or refrigerate in an airtight container until ready to serve.

> This salad is best if made a day in advance and will keep for up to 1 week if refrigerated in an airtight nonreactive container.

CHEF EMERIL'S SALAD

YIELD: 4 large or 6 to 8 side salads

INGREDIENTS

DRESSING

1/4 cup chopped scallions

1 teaspoon chopped parsley

1 teaspoon snipped chives (page 15)

1 teaspoon chopped tarragon

1 cup mayonnaise

1/4 cup buttermilk

2 teaspoons fresh lemon juice

1/2 teaspoon ground white pepper

1/2 teaspoon ground black pepper

1/2 teaspoon salt

SALAD

1/2 head iceberg lettuce, rinsed, patted dry, and torn into bite-size pieces (about 8 cups)

1 cup cubed cooked turkey

1 cup cubed cooked ham

1 cup cubed Cheddar cheese

1 cup cubed Swiss cheese

2 medium tomatoes, cut into wedges

2 hard-boiled eggs, chopped

TOOLS

Cutting board • chef's knife • kitchen scissors • juicer (optional) • measuring cups and spoons • food processor

Hey, did you know that a chef's salad is a "composed" salad? What that means is that instead of tossing everything together, you keep all the ingredients separate and place them decoratively on the plate for a knockout presentation. This salad packs a punch—and is a meal all on its own!

1 To make the dressing, combine the herbs in a food processor and pulse several times to mince. Add the mayonnaise and process until blended and smooth. Add the buttermilk, lemon juice, pepper, and salt. Pulse once or twice to blend well.

2 For the salad, arrange equal portions of the lettuce in the center of individual salad plates. Arrange equal amounts of the turkey, ham, cheese, and tomato wedges around the lettuce. Top each salad with some of the chopped egg and serve immediately. Serve the salad dressing on the side.

CAUTION

The food processor is a serious tool! Be extra careful when using it, and kids should never use this equipment unsupervised. I mean it! The blades are super-sharp and super-fast. NEVER turn this baby on without being sure the lid is on tightly. ALWAYS turn it off before taking the lid off. See pages 6–7 for more hints on how to use this handy tool safely.

TALK ABOUT A TACO SALAD

YIELD: 4 servings

INGREDIENTS

4 large burrito-size flour
    tortillas

2 tablespoons plus 2 teaspoons
    olive oil

1 to $1\frac{1}{4}$ pounds lean ground
    beef

$\frac{1}{2}$ cup finely chopped yellow
    onion

1 tablespoon tomato paste

2 teaspoons chopped garlic

2 teaspoons chili powder

1 teaspoon Baby Bam
    (page 25)

$\frac{1}{4}$ teaspoon salt

$\frac{1}{2}$ cup reduced-sodium chicken broth

2 cups shredded iceberg lettuce

$1\frac{1}{3}$ cups chopped tomato

$\frac{1}{2}$ cup grated cheese, such as sharp
    Cheddar or Monterey Jack

$\frac{1}{4}$ cup sour cream

Salsa (page 96) (optional)

Guacamole (page 97) (optional)

TOOLS

Cutting board • chef's knife • baking
sheet • parchment paper • $5\frac{1}{2}$-inch
stainless-steel mixing bowl •
pastry brush • oven mitts
or pot holders • wire
rack • 10-inch
skillet • wooden
spoon •
colander •
mixing bowl
• measuring
cups and
spoons •
box grater
• can
opener
(optional)

This salad makes a big impression—the bowls are made of flour tortillas that you bake in the oven! Now, this might sound like a bit of work, but it's really easy—it just takes a little time. If you're in a hurry, you can skip the homemade tortilla bowls and serve your salad on top of regular tortilla chips. Or you can make the bowls the day before and keep them in an airtight container so they keep their *crunch*.

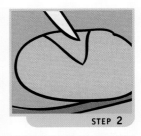
1   Position rack in center of oven and preheat the oven to 375°F.

2   To make the tortilla "bowls," cut a 3-inch wedge from each tortilla and discard. Line a baking sheet with parchment paper. Turn a stainless-steel mixing bowl upside down and place it on the parchment paper. Brush each side of the tortilla with 1 teaspoon of the olive oil. Drape each tortilla over the bowl (you will be able to do only one at a time), placing the cut ends together so that they now resemble an upside down shallow cone. Bake until crisp, about 10 minutes (tortilla will get crisper as it cools). Hint: If you have more than one small ovenproof bowl, you may be able to bake more than one tortilla at a time.

STEP 2

3   Using oven mitts or pot holders, remove the baking sheet from the oven and carefully transfer the crisp tortilla "bowl" to a wire rack to cool. Repeat with the remaining tortillas. Set aside.

4   While the tortilla "bowls" are baking, set the skillet over medium heat. Add the ground beef and cook, stirring occasionally, until brown, about 5 minutes.

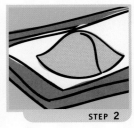

STEP 2

5   Remove from the heat and strain the beef in a colander set over a bowl to remove the fat. Discard the fat and return the beef to the pan and add the onion. Cook, stirring occasionally, until the onions are soft, about 3 minutes.

6   Add the tomato paste and garlic, stir to blend, and cook for about 30 seconds. Add the chili powder, Baby Bam, and salt. Stir to blend and add the chicken broth.

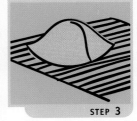

STEP 3

7   After about 1 minute, when the broth is reduced by half, remove from the heat and set aside to cool.

8   To assemble the salads, place a tortilla "bowl" right side up onto each of 4 plates. Place ½ cup of the ground beef mixture in the center of each tortilla "bowl." Top with ½ cup of the shredded lettuce, ⅓ cup of the tomatoes, 2 tablespoons of the cheese, and 1 tablespoon of the sour cream. Serve immediately, with Salsa and Guacamole, if desired.

STEP 8

Souper-Duper Soups and Sandwiches

FEEL-GOOD CHICKEN AND RICE SOUP

YIELD: 2 quarts, serving 6 to 8

INGREDIENTS

2 tablespoons olive oil

1½ cups chopped yellow onion

¾ cup chopped celery

¾ cup chopped carrots

2 teaspoons minced garlic

2 teaspoons salt

1 teaspoon Baby Bam (page 25)

1 teaspoon Emeril's Italian Essence or other dry Italian seasoning

1 bay leaf

⅛ teaspoon crushed red pepper

8 cups reduced-sodium chicken broth

¼ cup uncooked long-grain rice

10 to 12 ounces boneless, skinless chicken breasts, cut into ½-inch cubes

2 tablespoons chopped fresh parsley

TOOLS

6-quart saucepan with a lid • cutting board • chef's knife • measuring cups and spoons • wooden spoon • can opener (optional) • ladle • oven mitts or potholders

Everyone loves chicken and rice soup! And now you don't have to use the canned stuff—try making this at home for your friends and family. If you whip up a pot of this when someone you know is under the weather, I bet you they'll be feeling better quicker than you can say "BAM!"

1. Heat a large saucepan over high heat. Add the olive oil and, when hot, add the onion, celery, and carrots. Sauté until soft, about 4 minutes.

2. Add the garlic, salt, Baby Bam, Italian Essence, bay leaf, and crushed red pepper. Sauté for 2 more minutes. (Do not allow the garlic to brown.)

3. Add the chicken broth and bring to a boil. Cover and reduce the heat to medium-low and simmer for 20 minutes.

4. Add the rice and stir well to combine. Cover and continue to simmer for 20 minutes.

5. Add the chicken and cook until just cooked through, about 5 to 6 minutes.

6. Add the parsley, stir well, and serve.

HOT AND HEARTY MINESTRONE

YIELD: generous 2 quarts, serving 6 to 8

INGREDIENTS

1 tablespoon olive oil

2 slices bacon or pancetta

1 large leek, white and light green parts only, split in half and rinsed very well under running water, thinly sliced

1½ cups chopped yellow onion

6 cups reduced-sodium chicken broth

4 cups water

1 (28-ounce) can whole tomatoes, drained and chopped

¾ cup chopped carrots

¾ cup chopped celery

½ cup dried Great Northern beans, picked over (page 14) and soaked overnight or 1 (15-ounce) can white beans, drained and rinsed

1 Parmesan cheese rind, about 5 x 2 inches

1 teaspoon dried basil leaves

¼ teaspoon crushed red pepper

1¼ cups cubed zucchini

2 medium new potatoes, scrubbed and cubed (about 6 ounces or 1¼ cups cubed)

1 teaspoon Baby Bam (page 25)

1 teaspoon salt

2 cups packed fresh spinach leaves, washed, dried, and coarsely chopped

TOOLS

6-quart saucepan • cutting board • chef's knife • measuring cups and spoons • fork or tongs • wooden spoon • can opener (optional) • slotted spoon • ladle

This is one of my all-time favorite soups to make. It's one of those "feel-good" foods, and a pot of this simmering on the stovetop on a dreary day can revive just about anyone! Adding a piece of cheese rind while the soup is simmering is an authentic Italian trick that adds flavor, richness, and body. Try it!

1. In a large saucepan, heat the olive oil over medium-high heat. Add the bacon and fry until soft, using a fork or tongs to turn, about 2 minutes.

2. Add the leek and onion, and sauté until soft, about 4 minutes.

3. Add the chicken broth, water, tomatoes, carrots, celery, soaked beans, cheese rind, basil, and crushed red pepper. (If you are using canned beans, add them in step 5 along with the spinach.) Bring to a boil, then reduce the heat to medium-low and simmer for 30 minutes.

4. Add the zucchini, potatoes, Baby Bam, and salt. Return to a simmer and cook for 1 hour. If your soup gets too thick before serving, you may need to add a bit more water or chicken broth.

5. Add the spinach (and canned beans, if using) and cook for 15 minutes.

6. Remove the cheese rind with a slotted spoon, and serve.

Options: For a heartier minestrone, try adding about 1 cup of cubed French or Italian bread to the soup pot just before serving. Or do like the Italians do and add ¼ cup of small dried pasta to the pot when you add the spinach. Ditalini or another such small pasta shape works best.

If you live near an Italian market or gourmet shop, why not do things as they would in Italy and purchase some pancetta for your minestrone? Pancetta is nothing more than Italian bacon that is cured with salt and spices (like regular bacon), but unlike regular bacon, pancetta is not smoked. If you can't find pancetta, don't worry! I use regular bacon all the time in my minestrone, and it works great.

TORTELLINI IN BRODO

YIELD: 2 quarts, serving 6 to 8

INGREDIENTS

2 tablespoons olive oil

1½ cups chopped yellow onion

¾ cup chopped celery

¾ cup chopped carrots

2 teaspoons minced garlic

1 teaspoon Emeril's Italian Essence or other dry Italian seasoning

⅛ teaspoon crushed red pepper

8 cups reduced-sodium chicken broth

9 ounces fresh cheese-filled or 7 ounces dried cheese-filled tortellini

2 tablespoons minced parsley

Salt, to taste if necessary

½ cup finely grated Parmesan cheese

TOOLS

6-quart saucepan with a lid • cutting board • chef's knife • measuring cups and spoons • wooden spoon • can opener (optional) • box grater • ladle • oven mitts or pot holders

Man, let me tell you, a taste of this simple, classic Italian soup takes me back to Italy in a heartbeat! "In brodo" simply means "in soup." You can use either fresh or dried tortellini—whatever's available where you shop. Dried tortellini works just fine, but my preference is to use the fresh stuff. Mama mia!

1. Heat a large saucepan over high heat. Add the olive oil and, when hot, add the onion, celery, and carrots. Sauté until soft, about 4 minutes.

2. Add the garlic, Italian Essence, and crushed red pepper and sauté for 2 more minutes.

3. Add the chicken broth and bring to a boil. Cover, reduce the heat to medium-low, and simmer for 20 minutes.

4. Add the tortellini and cook for 5 minutes if using fresh; 15 minutes if using dried. The pasta should be al dente (see sidebar below).

5. Stir in the parsley, taste, and adjust the seasoning if necessary. Remove from heat and ladle into soup bowls.

6. Garnish each bowl with one tablespoon of the cheese. Serve immediately.

"Al dente" is an Italian expression that means "to the tooth" and is used to describe pasta or other foods that are cooked only until they offer slight resistance when bitten into, but are not overly soft or overcooked.

PIZZAZY PIZZA SANDWICHES

YIELD: 4 servings

INGREDIENTS

1¼ cups coarsely grated provolone cheese

1¼ cups coarsely grated mozzarella cheese

1 French baguette, about 20 inches long

½ cup Emeril's Kicked Up Tomato Sauce or your favorite red pasta sauce

¼ teaspoon Baby Bam (page 25)

¼ cup pepperoni slices (about 16 slices)

¼ cup finely grated Parmesan cheese

Crushed red pepper (optional)

TOOLS

Box grater • small mixing bowl • cutting board • serrated bread knife • measuring cups and spoons • small baking sheet • oven mitts or pot holders

Make up a big batch of these for your next party—friends and family will love them. The French bread bottom makes a great holder for all the cheese and other good stuff inside. Serve these with a nice green salad, such as the My Kinda Salad on page 64, and you've got yourself a meal!

82

1. Position rack in center of oven and preheat the oven to 325°F.

2. Combine the provolone and mozzarella cheeses in a small bowl.

3. Carefully cut the baguette into four 5-inch-long sections.

4. Cut off the top third of the bread horizontally and reserve top for another use. Using your fingers, gently scoop out and discard some of the soft, inner part of the bread, leaving a one-inch shell.

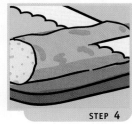

STEP 4

5. Spread the tomato sauce evenly among the bread shells, about 2 tablespoons for each sandwich, and sprinkle with the Baby Bam. Divide 2 cups of the cheese mixture among the 4 sandwiches and arrange the pepperoni slices evenly on top.

STEP 4

6. Place the sandwiches on a baking sheet and bake until the filling is heated through, about 20 minutes.

7. Using oven mitts or pot holders, remove the baking sheet from the oven, sprinkle the sandwiches evenly with the remaining cheese mixture, and return to the oven. Bake until the cheese melts, about 5 minutes.

STEP 5

8. Using oven mitts or pot holders, remove the baking sheet from the oven and sprinkle each sandwich evenly with some of the Parmesan cheese. If you like, you can sprinkle with crushed red pepper for a spicy Pizzazy Pizza Sandwich (a pinch should be just right).

HINT: Don't throw away any extra bread! You can use leftover or trimmed bread to make bread crumbs in a food processor.

FILL-'ER-UP FOCACCIA WITH ROASTED VEGGIES

YIELD: 8 sandwiches

INGREDIENTS

8 red bell peppers

$3/4$ cup plus 1 tablespoon extra-virgin olive oil

8 pieces of focaccia bread, roughly 4 by 5 inches each, or one recipe Focaccia (page 56) cut into 8 portions

6 tablespoons balsamic vinegar

$1/2$ teaspoon salt

$1/4$ teaspoon ground black pepper

1 pound fresh mozzarella, queso blanco, or provolone cheese, cut into $1/4$-inch slices

4 cups baby spinach, washed and patted dry

TOOLS

Large baking sheet • measuring cups and spoons • pastry brush • oven mitts or pot holders • large mixing bowl • plastic wrap • cutting board • chef's knife • serrated bread knife • small mixing bowl • whisk • spoon

These sandwiches are big enough for the heartiest appetites—put them in plastic wrap and bring them on picnics for a perfect "al fresco" lunchtime treat. You'll have a new favorite sandwich, for sure!

1. Position rack in center of oven and preheat the oven to 450°F. Brush the peppers with 1 tablespoon of the olive oil. Place them on an ungreased baking sheet and roast for 1 hour.

2. Using oven mitts or pot holders, remove the peppers from the oven and place them in a large mixing bowl. Cover with plastic wrap, and let them steam until cooled, about 30 to 40 minutes. Do not handle the hot peppers with your bare hands!

3. When cool, peel the skin from the peppers. Cut or tear open the peppers so that they lay flat, and remove the seeds, but try to keep each pepper in one piece. Set aside.

4. To make the sandwiches, slice each 4 by 5-inch piece of focaccia in half horizontally. Be careful here!

STEP 4

5. Separate the 16 pieces into 8 "top" pieces and 8 "bottom" pieces.

6. In a small mixing bowl, combine the remaining ¾ cup of olive oil, balsamic vinegar, salt, and pepper. Whisk to blend. Spread one tablespoon of this mixture on the cut side of each piece of bread.

7. Divide the mozzarella slices evenly among the 8 bottom halves, then top each half with 1 bell pepper and ½ cup of the spinach. Drizzle the remaining olive oil mixture over the spinach, and then place the top half of the bread over the spinach. Slice the sandwiches in half diagonally to serve.

STEP 7

OPEN-FACED ROAST TURKEY SANDWICHES

YIELD: 4 open-faced sandwiches and 1¾ cups gravy

INGREDIENTS

2 tablespoons unsalted butter

3 tablespoons all-purpose flour

¼ cup finely chopped yellow onion

1 tablespoon finely chopped celery

2 cups reduced-sodium chicken broth

1 teaspoon Baby Bam (page 25)

½ teaspoon salt

2 tablespoons mayonnaise

8 to 10 ounces thinly sliced roast turkey breast

4 slices home-style white bread

TOOLS

1½- to 2-quart saucepan • measuring cups and spoons • whisk • wooden spoon • cutting board • chef's knife • small ladle • oven mitts or pot holders • can opener (optional)

SAUTÉED MUSHROOMS

INGREDIENTS

2 tablespoons unsalted butter

8 ounces fresh white button mushrooms, wiped clean (page 14), stemmed, and thinly sliced

¼ teaspoon salt

Pinch of ground black pepper

TOOLS

8-inch skillet • cutting board • chef's knife • measuring spoons • wooden spoon • oven mitts or pot holders

Ah, this sandwich is *the* solution to what to do with leftover roast turkey. Do like I do and take the extra time to make the gravy and you'll take this sandwich up to the next notch in a very serious way. This will warm you through and through.

1. To make the gravy, heat a small saucepan over medium-high heat and melt the butter. Whisk in the flour to blend. With a wooden spoon, stir constantly until the mixture is the color of peanut butter, about 7 minutes. This is called making a roux.

2. Add the onion and celery and sauté until soft, about 2 minutes.

3. Whisk in the chicken broth, Baby Bam, and salt. Bring to a boil, reduce the heat to medium-low, and simmer until the mixture thickens and the floury taste is gone, about 20 minutes.

4. To assemble the sandwiches, spread about 1½ teaspoons of the mayonnaise on each slice of bread. Arrange equal amounts of the turkey on top of each slice of bread. Ladle equal amounts of the gravy (almost ½ cup each) over each open-faced sandwich. Serve immediately, topped with sautéed mushrooms if you like.

SAUTÉED MUSHROOMS

| DIRECTIONS | CAUTION | 👁 🔪 🔥 🧤 |

If you're a mushroom lover like me, why not add some sliced sautéed mushrooms to the top of your turkey sandwich?

1. In a medium skillet over high heat, melt the butter. Add the mushrooms, salt, and pepper, and sauté, stirring occasionally, until mushrooms are soft, have released their liquid, and are golden, about 3 minutes.

2. Divide the sautéed mushrooms evenly over the gravy among the tops of the sandwiches and serve.

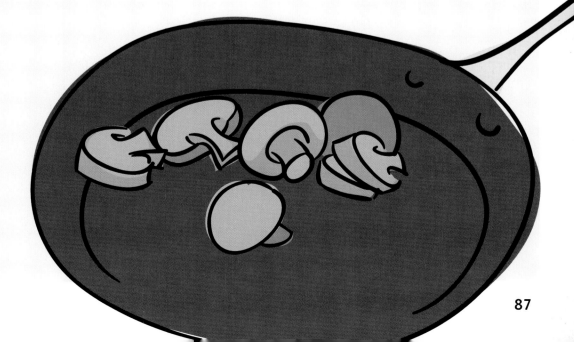

TOTALLY SLOPPY JOES

YIELD: 6 sandwiches

INGREDIENTS

1¼ to 1½ pounds lean ground beef

½ cup chopped yellow onion

1 tablespoon minced garlic

½ cup red wine vinegar

1 (14.5-ounce) can tomato sauce

2 tablespoons brown sugar

1 tablespoon Baby Bam (page 25)

½ teaspoon Emeril's Italian Essence or other dry Italian seasoning

¼ teaspoon ground black pepper

⅛ teaspoon salt

6 hamburger buns

TOOLS

12-inch skillet • wooden spoon • colander • cutting board • chef's knife • measuring cups and spoons • can opener • small baking sheet • oven mitts or pot holders

These make a super Father's Day treat for dads and granddads—I know when my friend Mallory makes them for her dad, Tony, she's the apple of his eye! They're the perfect thing to make ahead of time, too—all you need to do on the day of the party is heat up the sauce and buns and you're there! Add the Oven Crispy Cheese Fries on page 100 for a perfect combo.

1 Heat a skillet over medium heat. Add the ground beef and cook, stirring, until brown, about 5 minutes.

2 Strain the meat through a colander set over a bowl and return the meat to the pan. Discard the fat.

3 Add the onion and sauté until soft, about 3 minutes. Add the garlic and cook until fragrant, about 30 seconds.

4 Add the red wine vinegar, stirring to loosen the browned bits on the bottom of the pan, and cook for about 1 minute.

5 Add the tomato sauce, brown sugar, Baby Bam, Italian Essence, pepper, and salt. Stir to mix and bring to a gentle boil. Reduce the heat to medium-low and simmer for 15 minutes.

6 Meanwhile, position rack in center of oven and preheat the oven to 375°F. Place the buns on a baking sheet and warm in the oven for about 5 minutes.

7 Using oven mitts or pot holders, remove the baking sheet from the oven. Serve the Sloppy Joes by spooning ½ cup of the meat mixture onto the bottom half of each bun and top with the other half. Serve warm.

CHECK OUT MY CHICKEN SALAD SANDWICHES

YIELD: 4 super-stuffed sandwiches

INGREDIENTS

1 tablespoon white wine vinegar

1 tablespoon plus 1 teaspoon fresh lemon juice

1 teaspoon black peppercorns

$3/4$ teaspoon salt

2 sprigs fresh thyme

$1 1/4$ pounds boneless skinless chicken breasts (about $2 2/3$ cups cubed, cooked breast meat)

$3/4$ cup mayonnaise

$1/2$ cup minced celery

$2 1/2$ teaspoons minced parsley

$1/4$ teaspoon ground white pepper

8 slices home-style white bread

TOOLS

3-quart saucepan • measuring cups and spoons • slotted spoon • cutting board • chef's knife • large mixing bowl • wooden spoon • juicer (optional) • oven mitts or pot holders

These chicken salad sandwiches are super-yummy and great for entertaining guests. You can serve these on mini-croissants for parties or, if you really want to shake things up, check out the options I've suggested. You can make it different every time.

1. In a saucepan, combine the vinegar, 2 teaspoons of the lemon juice, peppercorns, ½ teaspoon salt, and thyme. Add the chicken breasts and enough water to cover by 1 inch. Bring to a boil over high heat. Skim off any scum that rises to the surface with a slotted spoon. Reduce the heat to medium low and simmer for 10 minutes.

2. Remove from the heat and allow the chicken to cool in the liquid for 45 minutes.

3. Once the chicken is cool, transfer to a cutting board and coarsely chop. Discard poaching liquid.

STEP 3

4. Transfer the chicken to a mixing bowl and add the mayonnaise, the remaining 2 teaspoons of lemon juice, celery, parsley, remaining ¼ teaspoon of salt, and white pepper. Use a wooden spoon to stir until thoroughly combined.

5. Divide the chicken salad among 4 slices of bread, about ⅔ cup per sandwich. Top with another slice of bread and serve immediately.

OPTIONS TO ADD TO SALAD

Minced scallions	Celery seeds	Toasted walnuts
Chopped fresh dill or tarragon	Sweet pickle relish	Grape halves

Snack
Attack

NACHO FIESTA

YIELD: 4 to 6 servings

INGREDIENTS

8 ounces tortilla chips (about 10 cups)

8 ounces Cheddar cheese ($1/2$ pound), shredded (about 2 cups)

8 ounces Monterey Jack cheese ($1/2$ pound), shredded (about 2 cups)

$1/4$ cup thinly sliced scallions

Salsa (page 96) (optional)

Guacamole (page 97) (optional)

$1/2$ cup sour cream (optional)

TOOLS

Measuring cups and spoons • cutting board • chef's knife • box grater • 9 x 13-inch baking dish or ovenproof platter • oven mitts or pot holders

This is a nacho lover's extravaganza: two layers of crispy tortilla chips with lots of gooey cheese in between—oh yeah, baby! These are seriously cheesy! Though I've suggested only homemade salsa, guacamole, and sour cream here, feel free to kick your nachos up by adding other extras as you like. Some of my favorites are cooked black beans, seasoned ground beef (see Talk about a Taco Salad on page 72), chopped cooked shrimp, and chicken. Use your imagination!

1 Position rack in center of oven and preheat the oven to 400°F.

2 In a 9 by 13-inch baking dish, spread half of the tortilla chips in one even layer and top with half of each cheese.

3 Repeat with another layer of chips and the remaining cheeses.

4 Bake until the cheese is melted and chips are crispy, about 8 to 10 minutes.

5 Using oven mitts or pot holders, remove the nachos from the oven, sprinkle with the scallions, and allow to cool slightly, about 2 minutes.

6 Serve either straight from the baking dish or divide among serving plates and serve with Salsa, Guacamole, and sour cream spooned over the top if desired.

(continued)

SALSA

DIRECTIONS | CAUTION 👁 🔪 🔌

YIELD: 1 cup

INGREDIENTS

3 ripe plum tomatoes (about ³/₄ pound) or 1 (14-ounce) can whole tomatoes, drained

¹/₄ cup chopped red or yellow onion

2 tablespoons minced fresh cilantro

1 clove garlic, minced

2 teaspoons fresh lime juice

¹/₄ teaspoon salt

¹/₄ teaspoon Emeril's Hot Sauce or other red hot sauce

TOOLS

Food processor • measuring cups and spoons • cutting board • chef's knife • juicer (optional) • can opener (optional) • plastic wrap (optional)

1 In the bowl of a food processor, combine all the ingredients and pulse until the salsa is mostly smooth but still slightly chunky, about 7 pulses. Be sure to follow processor safety instructions on pages 6–7.

2 Transfer to a bowl. Serve immediately or cover with plastic wrap and set aside until ready to serve the nachos.

GUACAMOLE

YIELD: About ¾ cup

INGREDIENTS

1 ripe avocado, peeled and cut into ½-inch pieces

1 tablespoon finely chopped yellow onion

1 clove garlic, minced

1 tablespoon minced fresh cilantro

2 teaspoons fresh lime juice

⅛ teaspoon salt

TOOLS

Measuring cups and spoons • cutting board • chef's knife • small mixing bowl • fork • juicer (optional) • plastic wrap (optional)

1. In a small mixing bowl, combine the avocado with the onion, garlic, cilantro, lime juice, and salt and mash with the back of a fork until mostly smooth.

2. Serve immediately, or cover with plastic wrap (pressed directly onto the surface of the guacamole) and refrigerate for up to 4 hours.

BLOW-YOU-AWAY BAGEL CHIPS

YIELD: 4 to 6 servings

INGREDIENTS

2 bagels

5 tablespoons olive oil

2 teaspoons minced garlic

1½ teaspoons Baby Bam (page 25)

½ teaspoon salt

TOOLS

Large baking sheet • parchment paper or aluminum foil • cutting board • serrated bread knife • measuring spoons • blender • pastry brush • oven mitts or pot holders • wire rack

Don't throw away leftover bagels—make chips! Why not whip up a batch of these for your next party? They're perfect for scooping up big tastes of Emeril's Con Queso (page 106), Fondue for You (page 104), Scoop-It-Up Spinach Dip (page 110), or the Mmmm-Hmmm Hummus (page 108). You can use homemade bagels from page 50, but store-bought bagels work just as well.

1. Position rack in center of oven and preheat the oven to 300°F. Line a baking sheet with parchment paper or aluminum foil and set aside.

2. Place the bagels on a cutting board and, using a serrated bread knife, slice downward to form ¼-inch slices. Place the bagel slices on the prepared baking sheet in 1 layer.

STEP 2

CAUTION It's best for an adult to help slice the bagels— watch those fingers!

3. In a blender, combine the oil and remaining ingredients and blend on medium speed until smooth. Remember to put the lid on tight before you turn the blender on.

4. Using a pastry brush, lightly coat one side of the bagel slices with the seasoned oil mixture.

STEP 4

5. Bake the bagel slices for 16 to 18 minutes, until golden brown and crisp.

6. Using oven mitts or pot holders, remove the pan from the oven and transfer to a wire rack to cool.

7. Chips may be made several days in advance, cooled completely, then stored in an airtight container for up to 2 weeks.

OVEN CRISPY CHEESE FRIES

YIELD: 4 to 6 servings

INGREDIENTS

2 teaspoons vegetable oil

2 large baking potatoes (about 1½ pounds), scrubbed

1 large egg white (page 18)

2 teaspoons Baby Bam (page 25)

8 ounces white Cheddar cheese (½ pound), grated (about 2 cups)

2 tablespoons thinly sliced scallions (optional)

Gravy (page 86) (optional)

TOOLS

Large nonstick baking sheet • measuring cups and spoons • cutting board • chef's knife • medium mixing bowl • whisk • slotted spoon • oven mitts or pot holders • metal spatula • box grater

You're not going to believe how crispy these French fries are! The secret is coating them with beaten egg white and baking them in the oven. Since they're not deep-fried in oil, they're a healthier treat too. These go great with burgers, hot dogs, and all your favorite sandwiches!

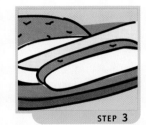
1 Position rack in center of oven and preheat the oven to 425°F.

2 Grease a large nonstick baking sheet with the vegetable oil.

3 Pat the potatoes dry and slice lengthwise into ½-inch thick slices.

4 Turn each slice flat and slice again lengthwise into even fries, ½-inch thick.

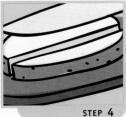

STEP 3

5 In a medium mixing bowl, whisk the egg white until very light and foamy.

6 Add the potatoes to the egg white and toss to coat evenly. Remove potatoes with a slotted spoon.

7 Spread the coated potatoes on the prepared baking sheet, so the fries are not touching one another. Bake for 10 minutes.

8 Using oven mitts or pot holders, remove the baking sheet from the oven. Sprinkle the potatoes with half the Baby Bam. With a metal spatula, scrape the potatoes from the baking sheet and flip them over. Sprinkle with the remaining teaspoon of Baby Bam.

STEP 4

9 With oven mitts or pot holders, return the baking sheet to the oven and bake for 20 minutes, until golden brown and crispy.

10 Using oven mitts or pot holders, remove the baking sheet from the oven and sprinkle the potatoes with the cheese.

11 With oven mitts or pot holders, return the baking sheet to the oven until the cheese is melted, about 3 minutes.

12 Using oven mitts or pot holders, remove the baking sheet from the oven and sprinkle the potatoes with the scallions (optional). Carefully transfer the potatoes with the spatula to a large serving plate or individual plates.

13 Serve immediately, with gravy (page 86), if desired.

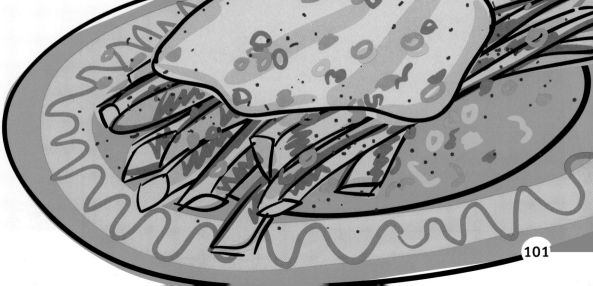

CHEESY PUFF PASTRY—WITH A TWIST

YIELD: About 30 twists

INGREDIENTS

1 sheet frozen puff pastry (one half of a 17.3-ounce package)

Butter or nonstick cooking spray if using aluminum foil

$\frac{1}{3}$ cup grated Parmesan cheese

2 tablespoons extra-virgin olive oil

2 teaspoons Baby Bam (page 25)

2 teaspoons Emeril's Italian Essence or other dry Italian seasoning

2 teaspoons minced garlic

1 large egg

All-purpose flour, for dusting

TOOLS

3 large baking sheets • parchment paper or aluminum foil • kitchen towel • cutting board • chef's knife • box grater • measuring cups and spoons • 2 small mixing bowls • wooden spoon • fork • rolling pin • pastry brush • spoon • pizza wheel (optional) • oven mitts or pot holders

These are a super snack or a wonderful party hors d'oeuvre. The store-bought puff pastry makes it easy for you to experiment with your own combination of spices and cheeses. My version will get you started, but you can take over from there!

1 Position rack in the center of oven and preheat oven to 400°F.

2 Line three large baking sheets with parchment paper. (Alternatively, line the baking sheets with aluminum foil and lightly grease with butter or nonstick cooking spray.)

3 Thaw the pastry sheet at room temperature covered by a clean kitchen towel, about 30 minutes.

STEP 9

4 While the pastry is thawing, combine the cheese, olive oil, Baby Bam, Italian Essence, and garlic in a small mixing bowl. Stir well to combine.

5 In another small mixing bowl, beat the egg with a fork and set aside.

6 On a lightly floured surface, gently unfold the pastry.

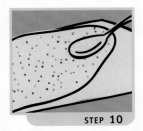
STEP 10

7 Dust the pastry lightly with flour and, using a rolling pin, roll into a 14 by 10-inch rectangle.

8 Using a pastry brush, brush the top of the pastry with the beaten egg.

9 Cut the pastry in half to form two 7 by 10-inch rectangles.

10 With the back of a spoon, spread the herb-cheese mixture evenly across one rectangle.

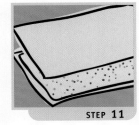
STEP 11

11 Lay the second rectangle across the cheese-coated piece, egg side down.

12 With the rolling pin, lightly roll the two sheets together to seal.

13 With a large knife, cut the sheets crosswise into strips, about ⅓ inch wide each. (Alternatively, you can use a pizza wheel to cut the strips.)

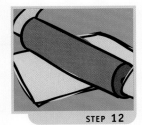
STEP 12

14 One at a time, grab the ends of each strip and twist in opposite directions to form a spiral.

15 Transfer the twists to the prepared baking sheets.

16 Bake the twists until light golden brown, about 10 minutes.

17 Using oven mitts or pot holders, remove the baking sheets from the oven and let the twists cool on the sheets until cool enough to handle.

STEP 13

18 Serve the twists either warm or at room temperature.

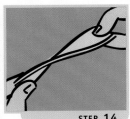
STEP 14

FONDUE FOR YOU

YIELD: 2 cups, serving 4 to 6

INGREDIENTS

½ pound Emmentaler cheese, rind discarded, cut into small cubes (1 cup)

½ pound Gruyère cheese, rind discarded, cut into small cubes (1 cup)

1 tablespoon cornstarch

2 tablespoons unsalted butter

4 ounces fresh button mushrooms, wiped clean (page 14), stemmed, and chopped (1 cup chopped)

2 tablespoons minced shallots

¾ cup apple cider

¼ cup water

1 tablespoon fresh lemon juice

½ teaspoon freshly ground black pepper

¼ teaspoon salt

Crusty French or Italian bread, cut into cubes, for dipping (optional)

Apple slices, for dipping (optional)

Boiled new potatoes, cut into cubes, for dipping (optional)

Pear slices, for dipping (optional)

TOOLS

Cutting board • chef's knife • measuring cups and spoons • medium mixing bowl • medium saucepan • wooden spoon • juicer (optional) • fondue pot or chafing dish • long-handled forks or skewers • oven mitts or pot holders

Fondue is fun! With everyone huddled around a pot of warm, melted cheese—life doesn't get much better than this! This recipe calls for a fondue pot, but if you don't own one, don't worry! A chafing dish works too. Whatever you use, make sure the flame isn't too high—only a little heat is needed to keep the fondue at just the right temperature. Specialty cheeses may be hard to find, but simple Swiss does the trick.

1. In a medium bowl, combine the cheeses and cornstarch and toss to coat evenly. Set aside.

2. In a heavy medium saucepan, melt the butter over medium heat.

3. Add the mushrooms and cook, stirring, until golden brown and most of their liquid has evaporated, about 5 minutes.

4. Add the shallots and cook, stirring, until soft, about 1 minute.

5. Add the cider, water, and lemon juice, and bring to a simmer.

6. Reduce the heat to medium-low and add the cheese-cornstarch mixture in 3 additions, stirring constantly and adding more cheese as the previous addition has melted.

7. Once all the cheese has been added, add the pepper and salt and stir.

8. Remove the pan from the heat.

9. Carefully pour the fondue into a fondue pot for serving, being sure to follow the manufacturer's instructions.

10. Serve hot with dipping items of choice.

CAUTION

Be careful when eating the items dipped in the hot cheese—it can get really hot! Most fondue pots come with long-handled forks or skewers that make dipping easier and safer. Be sure an adult helps you with this.

EMERIL'S CON QUESO

YIELD: 3 cups, serving 6 to 8

INGREDIENTS

2 tablespoons vegetable oil

1 cup chopped yellow onion

1 teaspoon Baby Bam (page 25)

1 cup chopped seeded tomato, (optional)

1 teaspoon minced garlic

8 ounces white Cheddar cheese (½ pound), shredded (about 2 cups)

8 ounces Monterey Jack cheese (½ pound), shredded (about 2 cups)

1 cup canned, chopped mild green chiles

3 tablespoons sour cream

1 teaspoon ground white pepper

¼ teaspoon salt

Tortilla chips, for serving

TOOLS

3½-quart saucepan • cutting board • chef's knife • measuring cups and spoons • wooden spoon • box grater • can opener • oven mitts or pot holders

Man oh man, talk about a fiesta! Mild chile peppers make this Queso tasty for most folks. But hey, if you don't like chiles at all, skip them or add chopped bell pepper instead. If you're like me and enjoy kicking up the heat level a couple of notches, try using chiles labeled hot or medium hot. A little spice in your life is a good thing!

| CAUTION 👁 🔪 🔥 🧤

1. Heat the vegetable oil in a medium saucepan over medium heat until hot, about 1 minute.

2. Add the onion and Baby Bam and cook, stirring, until soft, about 5 minutes.

3. Stir in the tomato, if using, and garlic and cook, stirring, for another 2 minutes.

4. Reduce the heat to medium-low and add the cheeses and chiles. Cook, stirring constantly, until the cheese melts, about 2 minutes.

5. Stir in the sour cream, white pepper, and salt and serve immediately with tortilla chips.

MMMM-HMMM HUMMUS

YIELD: About 2 cups, serving 4 to 6

INGREDIENTS

1 (15-ounce) can chickpeas, drained and rinsed well in a colander set in a sink

1/4 cup extra-virgin olive oil

1/4 cup chopped yellow onion

1/4 cup water

1/4 cup tahini

1 tablespoon fresh lemon juice, plus extra for serving, if desired

1 1/2 teaspoons red wine vinegar

1 1/2 teaspoons Baby Bam (page 25)

3/4 teaspoon ground cumin

3/4 teaspoon salt

1/2 teaspoon minced garlic

1/8 teaspoon ground cayenne pepper

Pita bread, pita chips, Blow-You-Away Bagel Chips (page 98), or vegetables, for dipping (optional)

TOOLS

Food processor • can opener • colander • juicer (optional) • cutting board • chef's knife • measuring cups and spoons • rubber spatula • airtight container

Hummus is a wonderful Middle Eastern dip made from chickpeas. Try it—it's delicious! I usually stay away from canned beans, but chickpeas are an exception—especially for this recipe. I like to eat my hummus with pita chips—but it also goes great with the Blow-You-Away Bagel Chips on page 98. If you're a lemon lover like I am, you might try squeezing a little extra lemon juice over the top just before serving!

1 In the bowl of a food processor combine the chickpeas with 3 tablespoons of the olive oil, the onion, water, tahini, lemon juice, red wine vinegar, 1 teaspoon of the Baby Bam, the cumin, salt, garlic, and cayenne pepper. Process until the mixture is combined and mostly smooth, about 1 minute. Be sure to follow processor safety directions on pages 6–7.

2 Turn the processor off and carefully remove the lid and blade. Using a rubber spatula, remove the hummus from the bowl of the processor, transfer to an airtight container, and refrigerate until chilled, at least $1\frac{1}{2}$ to 2 hours and up to several days in advance.

3 When ready to serve, stir the hummus and transfer to a shallow serving bowl. Drizzle with the remaining tablespoon of extra-virgin olive oil and sprinkle with the remaining $\frac{1}{2}$ teaspoon Baby Bam.

4 Serve with pita bread, pita chips, Blow-You-Away Bagel Chips, or vegetables for dipping.

> Tahini is a paste made from ground sesame seeds. You'll find it in health-food stores and in many regular grocery stores. In certain parts of the world this spread is as popular as peanut butter is in the United States. It's packed full of protein and makes a wonderful addition to a vegetarian diet.

SCOOP-IT-UP SPINACH DIP

YIELD: About 2½ cups, serving 4 to 6

INGREDIENTS

1½ pounds fresh spinach, washed and stems removed, or 1 (10-ounce) package frozen spinach, thawed, drained, and squeezed dry

2 tablespoons butter

1 tablespoon finely chopped yellow onion

1½ teaspoons minced garlic

2 tablespoons all-purpose flour

1 cup heavy cream

¼ cup milk

½ cup finely grated Parmesan cheese

1 teaspoon fresh lemon juice

1 teaspoon Baby Bam (page 25)

¼ teaspoon salt

3 tablespoons sour cream

¼ cup grated Monterey Jack or pecorino Romano cheese

Tortilla chips or other chips of choice, for dipping

TOOLS

Measuring cups and spoons • 6-quart saucepan • oven mitts or pot holders • colander • cutting board • chef's knife • medium saucepan • wooden spoon • whisk • juicer (optional) • box grater

Without a doubt, this is my favorite way to eat spinach. It gets all creamy and cheesy and, oh, don't make me talk about it! It's a serious food-of-love thing. I like to eat it with crispy tortilla chips, but hey, just about anything would taste great dipped in this stuff, especially the homemade Blow-You-Away Bagel Chips on page 98.

1 If using fresh spinach, bring a large saucepan filled ⅔ full with water to a rolling boil.

2 Add the spinach and cook for 1 to 2 minutes, or just until spinach wilts and water returns to a boil. Using oven mitts or pot holders, remove from the heat and strain the spinach in a colander set in the sink. Rinse under cold running water until cool.

3 If using frozen spinach, skip steps 1 and 2. Let the spinach thaw and drain in a colander set in the sink.

4 Using your hands, squeeze the spinach to remove as much liquid as possible. You should have about 1½ cups of spinach.

5 Place spinach on a cutting board and chop finely. Set aside.

6 In a heavy medium saucepan, melt the butter over medium-high heat. Add the onion and cook until soft, about 3 minutes. Add the garlic and cook until fragrant, about 1 to 2 minutes. Do not allow garlic to brown.

7 Add the flour and stir to combine. Cook, stirring constantly, until mixture is a light-blond color, about 1 to 2 minutes.

8 Whisk in the heavy cream and milk, little by little, until the mixture is smooth. Continue to cook until the mixture comes to a boil and thickens, about 2 minutes.

9 Reduce the heat to medium-low and simmer for 3 to 4 minutes.

10 Add the Parmesan cheese, lemon juice, Baby Bam, and salt, and stir to combine well.

11 Remove from the heat. Add the sour cream, chopped spinach, and Monterey Jack or pecorino Romano cheese and stir until the cheese is melted.

12 Serve immediately, with tortilla chips or other dipping chips of choice.

Time for Dinner!

CHAPTER 6

VERY VEGGIE LASAGNA

YIELD: 10 servings

INGREDIENTS

2 (15-ounce) containers ricotta cheese

2 tablespoons chopped fresh basil

2 tablespoons chopped fresh thyme

2 tablespoons chopped fresh parsley

4 teaspoons extra-virgin olive oil

2 teaspoons salt

1 teaspoon ground black pepper

$\frac{1}{4}$ cup olive oil

3 cups sliced mushrooms

$1\frac{1}{4}$ cups finely chopped yellow onion

1 tablespoon Emeril's Italian Essence or other dry Italian seasoning

2 teaspoons minced garlic

1 head broccoli, cut into florets (about 2 cups)

2 carrots, peeled and coarsely chopped (about 2 cups)

$1\frac{1}{2}$ cups coarsely chopped red bell pepper

$1\frac{1}{2}$ cups coarsely chopped yellow bell pepper

$1\frac{1}{2}$ cups coarsely chopped green bell pepper

$1\frac{1}{2}$ cups coarsely chopped yellow squash

$1\frac{1}{2}$ cups coarsely chopped zucchini

2 (28-ounce) cans whole peeled tomatoes, undrained

2 tablespoons tomato paste

2 tablespoons sugar

12 to 15 large uncooked lasagna noodles

5 cups grated mozzarella cheese (about $1\frac{1}{4}$ pounds)

$\frac{1}{2}$ cup grated Parmesan cheese

TOOLS

Measuring cups and spoons • vegetable peeler • cutting board • chef's knife • medium mixing bowl • wooden spoon • 6-quart pot • can opener • large mixing bowl • 10 x 14-inch roasting pan • rubber spatula • box grater • aluminum foil • oven mitts or pot holders

We used almost a full box of lasagna noodles to make this lasagna. You might need more or less, depending on the size of your pan and how closely you space the noodles. We used a lot of different vegetables and had fun choosing our favorites and what was freshest at the market. You can leave some of these veggies out, add some others, or use more of the ones your family likes best. Just make sure that you have 12 total cups of vegetables for the sauce. Lots of ingredients means everybody can help out.

1. Position rack in center of oven and preheat the oven to 375°F.

2. In a medium bowl, combine the ricotta cheese, basil, thyme, parsley, extra-virgin olive oil, 1 teaspoon of the salt, and ½ teaspoon of the black pepper. Stir to combine and set aside.

3. In a large pot, heat the olive oil over medium-high heat. Add the mushrooms, onion, and Italian Essence and cook, stirring, until the onions are soft and the mushrooms are wilted and have released their juices, about 5 minutes.

4. Add the garlic and cook, stirring, for 1 minute.

5. Add all the remaining vegetables except the tomatoes, and cook, stirring, until they start to soften, about 10 minutes.

STEP 6

6. In a large bowl, using your fingers, crush the tomatoes into pieces.

7. Add the crushed tomatoes, tomato paste, and sugar to the pot, and cook, stirring, until thick and most of the liquid has evaporated, about 15 minutes.

8. Add the remaining teaspoon of salt and remaining ½ teaspoon of pepper and stir well.

9. Remove the pot from the heat.

STEP 10

10. Spread 3 cups of the tomato-vegetable sauce evenly over the bottom of a large roasting pan. Arrange one layer of lasagna noodles on top, being careful not to overlap them.

11. Spoon 1 cup of the ricotta cheese mixture over the noodles, spreading evenly with a rubber spatula.

12. Sprinkle 1 cup of the mozzarella cheese evenly over the ricotta.

STEP 11

13. Repeat the layering with the remaining ingredients, for a total of 3 complete layers, ending with the remaining 2 cups of mozzarella cheese on top.

14. Sprinkle the Parmesan cheese over the mozzarella cheese.

15. Cover the pan tightly with aluminum foil and bake for 1½ hours.

16. Using oven mitts or pot holders, carefully remove the pan from the oven and remove the foil. Do not remove the foil with bare fingers.

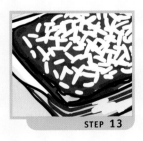

STEP 13

17. Using oven mitts or pot holders, return the pan to the oven and bake the lasagna until golden brown and bubbly, about 15 minutes.

18. Using oven mitts or pot holders, remove the lasagna from the oven and let cool for 10 minutes before serving.

CAUTION

Hey, be extra careful with this dish. When all assembled, it's very heavy and very hot and bubbly from cooking so long. An adult should be in the kitchen to help.

FETTUCCINE ALFREDO MY WAY

YIELD: 6 servings

INGREDIENTS

1 pound fettuccine, tagliatelle, or other wide ribbon noodles

1 tablespoon plus 1 teaspoon salt

2 tablespoons unsalted butter

1 tablespoon olive oil

$\frac{1}{4}$ cup small diced smoked cured ham (optional)

$\frac{1}{2}$ cup finely chopped yellow onion

1 tablespoon minced garlic

2 cups heavy cream

$\frac{1}{2}$ cup green peas, defrosted if frozen (optional)

$\frac{1}{2}$ teaspoon freshly ground black pepper

1 cup grated Parmesan cheese

2 tablespoons chopped fresh parsley (optional)

TOOLS

6-quart pot • wooden spoon • 12-inch skillet • cutting board • chef's knife • measuring cups and spoons • oven mitts or pot holders • colander • large bowl • box grater

Man, this is one of my all-time favorite classic pasta dishes. I make this at home for my family all the time. Depending on who's coming to dinner, I might add a little chopped ham and some peas to jazz it up. These additions make it more like another great Italian classic, pasta carbonara, but hey—it's deliciously good and creamy any way you make it! Watch your family dig in.

116

1. Bring a large pot of water to a boil.

2. Add the pasta and 1 tablespoon of the salt. Return to a boil and cook the pasta until al dente (page 81), stirring occasionally to prevent the noodles from sticking, about 10 to 12 minutes.

3. Meanwhile, melt the butter and heat the oil in a large skillet over medium heat.

4. Add the ham, if desired, and cook, stirring, for 1 minute.

5. Add the onion and cook, stirring, for 2 minutes.

6. Add the garlic, and cook, stirring, for 30 seconds.

7. Add the heavy cream and bring to a boil. Cook until the volume is reduced by half, about 5 minutes. If desired, add the peas. Add the remaining teaspoon of salt and the pepper, and stir well.

8. Using oven mitts or pot holders, drain the pasta in a colander set in the sink and place the pasta in a large bowl.

9. Pour the sauce over the pasta. Add the cheese and toss to coat.

10. If desired, add the parsley and adjust the seasoning to taste.

11. Serve immediately.

PASTA PRIMAVERA

YIELD: 8 servings

INGREDIENTS

1/2 cup cubed carrots

1/2 cup asparagus, sliced crosswise into 1/2-inch pieces

1 pound orecchiette pasta or other pasta

1 tablespoon plus 1 teaspoon salt

2 tablespoons unsalted butter

2 tablespoons olive oil

1/2 cup chopped yellow onion

1 tablespoon minced garlic

1 cup cubed zucchini

1 cup cubed yellow squash

1/2 cup chopped tomato

1/2 cup frozen green peas

1/2 teaspoon ground black pepper

1/4 cup extra-virgin olive oil

2 tablespoons chopped fresh parsley

1/2 cup grated Parmesan cheese (optional garnish)

TOOLS

6-quart pot • 1- to 2-quart saucepan • cutting board • chef's knife • measuring cups and spoons • wooden spoon • oven mitts or pot holders • colander • small ladle • large mixing bowl • small cup • plastic wrap or kitchen towel • 12-inch skillet • box grater (optional)

This is a wonderful dish to make in the springtime, when the new vegetables at the market are all so sweet and tender. I think you'll really like making this with one of my favorite pasta shapes— *orecchiette*. The word *orecchiette* means "little ears" in Italian, and this disk-shaped pasta is perfect for holding little bites of vegetables. But choose the shape that you like best!

1. Bring a large pot of water to a boil.

2. As the pasta water is heating, bring a small saucepan of water to a boil.

3. Add the carrots and asparagus to the small saucepan and blanch for 2 minutes (page 21).

4. Using oven mitts or pot holders, remove the small saucepan from the heat and pour the carrots and asparagus away from you into a colander set in the sink. Rinse under cold running water to refresh.

5. While cooking the vegetables, add the pasta and 1 tablespoon of the salt to the large pot of boiling water.

6. Return to a boil and cook the pasta until al dente (page 81), stirring occasionally, about 12 to 15 minutes.

7. Turn the stove off, and with a small ladle, transfer $\frac{1}{4}$ cup of the cooking liquid to a small cup and set aside.

8. Using oven mitts or pot holders, drain the rest of the pot away from you into a colander set in the sink.

9. Place the pasta in a large bowl with the $\frac{1}{4}$ cup cooking liquid and cover with plastic wrap or a clean kitchen towel to keep warm.

10. In a large skillet over medium-high heat, melt the butter and, when hot, add the olive oil.

11. Add the onion and cook, stirring, for 2 minutes.

12. Add the garlic, and cook, stirring, for 30 seconds.

13. Add the zucchini and squash, and cook, stirring, for 3 minutes.

14. Add the cooked carrots and asparagus, and cook, stirring, for 1 minute.

15. Add the tomato, peas, the remaining teaspoon of salt, and the pepper. Stir and remove from the heat.

16. Pour the vegetables over the pasta in the bowl.

17. Drizzle with the extra-virgin olive oil, add the parsley, and toss to coat evenly.

18. Sprinkle, if you like, with the Parmesan cheese.

19. Serve immediately.

SAY "CHEESE" ENCHILADAS

YIELD: 12 enchiladas, serving 6 to 12

INGREDIENTS

5 tablespoons vegetable oil

1 (28-ounce) can peeled whole tomatoes

2/3 cup chopped yellow onion

1/2 teaspoon ground cumin

1/2 teaspoon dried oregano

1/2 teaspoon Baby Bam (page 25)

2 teaspoons minced garlic

1/2 teaspoon salt

1/2 teaspoon freshly ground black pepper

12 corn tortillas

8 ounces white Cheddar cheese (1/2 pound), grated (about 2 cups)

8 ounces yellow Cheddar cheese (1/2 pound), grated (about 2 cups)

1/3 cup finely chopped yellow onion (optional)

2 tablespoons chopped fresh cilantro (optional garnish)

TOOLS

9 x 13-inch baking dish • can opener • blender • 2 medium skillets • measuring cups and spoons • cutting board • chef's knife • wooden spoon • small bowl • pastry brush • tongs • large plate • box grater • medium bowl • oven mitts or pot holders

I don't know about you, but when it comes to enchiladas, the simple cheese ones are my favorites. Sometimes simple is just better, and this is definitely one of those times. I've used two different kinds of Cheddar here, but Monterey Jack and Cheddar is another option. This is a good dish for several people to make together—one person can grate the cheese while another chops, and someone else can fold up the tortillas with all the fixings inside. Get everybody cooking!

DIRECTIONS

CAUTION

1. Position rack in center of oven and preheat the oven to 400°F.

2. Lightly grease a large baking dish with 1 tablespoon of the oil. Set aside.

3. In a blender, puree the tomatoes on high speed.

4. In a medium skillet, heat 2 tablespoons of the remaining oil over medium-high heat. Add the onion, cumin, oregano, and Baby Bam and cook, stirring, until soft, about 4 minutes.

5. Add the garlic and cook, stirring, for 1 minute.

6. Add the pureed tomatoes. Reduce the heat to medium-low and cook, stirring, until slightly thickened, about 5 minutes.

7. Season with the salt and pepper and stir.

8. Reduce the heat to very low. Simmer to keep warm, stirring occasionally, while you assemble the enchiladas.

9. Heat a second medium skillet over low heat.

10. Place the remaining 2 tablespoons of the oil in a small bowl or dish.

11. With a pastry brush, lightly brush both sides of each tortilla with the oil.

12. Place one tortilla at a time in the skillet until just warm and softened, about 2 to 5 seconds per side.

13. Remove tortilla with tongs and place it on a large plate. Continue with the remaining tortillas and oil.

14. Combine the white and yellow Cheddar cheeses in a medium bowl.

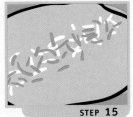
STEP 15

15. Sprinkle 1/4 cup of the mixed cheese in a line along the middle of each tortilla.

16. If using the finely chopped raw onion, sprinkle a heaping teaspoon into each tortilla.

17. Fold one side toward the middle to enclose the filling, then roll up the tortilla to form a cylinder.

STEP 17

18. Place tortillas seam side down in a single layer in the prepared baking dish.

19. Pour the tomato sauce over the filled enchiladas, spreading with the back of a spoon to distribute evenly.

20. Sprinkle the remaining 1 cup of cheese over the top of the enchiladas.

21. Bake until bubbly, about 10 to 12 minutes.

22. Using oven mitts or pot holders, remove the baking dish from the oven and let sit for 5 minutes before serving.

STEP 20

23. To serve, divide enchiladas among plates and garnish, if desired, with the cilantro.

GARLIC LOVERS' POT ROAST

YIELD: 6 to 8 servings

INGREDIENTS

1 boneless beef chuck roast (about 3 pounds)

10 cloves garlic, peeled and cut in half lengthwise

2 teaspoons salt

1/2 teaspoon ground black pepper

2 tablespoons vegetable oil

2/3 cup water

TOOLS

Cutting board • paring knife • measuring spoons • Dutch oven or heavy skillet or saucepan with lid • meat fork or other long-handled fork • oven mitts or potholders

My friend Charlotte's grandmother, MaMa LaChute, showed me how to make this simply deliciously gaaaaahlicky pot roast, and you'll be glad I shared this recipe with you. It's easier than most, since it is cooked entirely on top of the stove. You'll end up with meat that melts in your mouth and delicious pan juices to go with it. The adults can make the cuts in the meat but then let the kids have the fun of sticking the garlic into the roast.

1. Using the tip of a sharp paring knife, make 20 evenly spaced small slits about 1½ inches deep all over the pot roast.

2. Using your fingers, insert the garlic cloves as deep into the meat as possible.

3. Season the roast on all sides with the salt and pepper. Wash hands well before continuing.

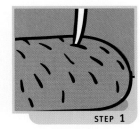

STEP 1

4. Heat a Dutch oven over high heat. Add the oil and, when hot, use the meat fork to add the roast. Use oven mitts or pot holders and be careful here! The pan and oil will be very hot and the meat will really sizzle when you add it.

5. Sear the meat on all sides until very well browned, about 4 to 6 minutes per side. Don't be afraid to let the roast get *very* brown—this is where a lot of the flavor comes from.

STEP 2

6. When the roast is evenly browned on all sides, carefully add the water and cover the pot.

7. Reduce the heat to low/medium-low and cook the roast until it is very tender, about 3 to 3½ hours, turning 2 or 3 times during the entire cooking time. Check occasionally to make sure that there is always a little liquid on the bottom of the pan. If necessary, add more water.

STEP 4

8. When the roast is very tender, carefully transfer to a serving platter with a meat fork. Use oven mitts or pot holders and have an adult help if this seems too hard for you to do alone.

9. Slice or pull meat apart into serving pieces and serve with the pan juices drizzled over the top.

> The secrets to this roast are not to add too much liquid at any one time and to let it cook long and real slow. Be patient—it's worth it!

MIGHTY MEATY MEATLOAF

YIELD: 8 servings

INGREDIENTS

2 tablespoons vegetable oil

1 cup chopped yellow onion

$\frac{1}{2}$ cup chopped celery

$\frac{1}{2}$ cup chopped green bell pepper

1 tablespoon minced garlic

$1\frac{1}{2}$ teaspoons salt

$\frac{1}{2}$ teaspoon dried basil

$\frac{1}{2}$ teaspoon dried thyme

$\frac{1}{2}$ teaspoon ground black pepper

$1\frac{1}{2}$ pounds ground beef

$\frac{1}{2}$ pound ground pork

$\frac{1}{2}$ pound ground veal

2 eggs

$\frac{1}{2}$ cup heavy cream

$\frac{1}{4}$ cup ketchup

2 teaspoons Baby Bam (page 25)

$1\frac{1}{2}$ teaspoons Dijon mustard

1 teaspoon Worcestershire sauce

$\frac{2}{3}$ cup fine dried bread crumbs

GLAZE

$\frac{1}{2}$ cup ketchup

2 tablespoons light brown sugar

1 teaspoon Worcestershire sauce

$\frac{1}{4}$ teaspoon Emeril's Hot Sauce or other red hot sauce (optional)

TOOLS

8-inch skillet • measuring cups and spoons • cutting board • chef's knife • wooden spoon • large mixing bowl • medium mixing bowl • whisk • 9 x 5 x 3-inch loaf pan • small bowl • small spoon • oven mitts or pot holders

This meatloaf is mighty meaty indeed! With three different types of meat, it's hard to go wrong with this one. We've topped it with a tomatoey glaze that'll knock your socks off. I promise! Make this for a family supper and hey, if you're lucky enough to have leftovers, try a meatloaf sandwich the next day for lunch. Talk about good!

1   Position rack in center of oven and preheat the oven to 350°F.

2   Heat the vegetable oil in a skillet over medium heat.

3   Add the onion, celery, bell pepper, garlic, salt, basil, thyme, and black pepper. Cook, stirring, until the onions are soft and lightly golden, about 6 minutes.

4   Remove from the heat and set aside to cool.

5   In a large mixing bowl, combine the ground beef, pork, and veal with a wooden spoon or with clean hands. Be sure to wash up afterward as directed (page 5).

STEP 5

6   In a medium mixing bowl, combine the eggs, heavy cream, ketchup, Baby Bam, Dijon mustard, and Worcestershire sauce, and whisk to combine.

7   Add the egg mixture to the meat mixture along with the cooled vegetables and bread crumbs. Mix with your hands or a wooden spoon until thoroughly combined.

8   Transfer the mixture to a 9 by 5 by 3-inch loaf pan. Using your fingers or the back of the wooden spoon, smooth the top into a rounded loaf shape.

STEP 8

9   To make the glaze, combine the ketchup, brown sugar, Worcestershire, and hot sauce, if desired, in a small bowl. Stir to blend. Spread the mixture evenly over the top of the meatloaf.

10   Bake the meatloaf for 1 hour and 15 minutes.

11   Using oven mitts or pot holders, remove the pan from the oven and set aside to cool for 10 minutes before serving.

12   Using oven mitts or pot holders, carefully tilt the pan away from you and drain off the excess grease from the pan. An adult should help you here. Be careful, hot grease can really burn. Slice to serve.

STEP 12

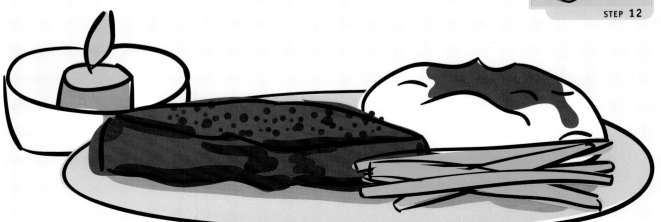

PENNE WITH ITALIAN SAUSAGE

YIELD: 6 to 8 servings

INGREDIENTS

1 pound penne pasta

1 tablespoon plus 1 teaspoon salt

1 pound sweet or mild Italian sausage, removed from the casings (page 18) and coarsely crumbled or chopped

2 cups thinly sliced yellow onion

1 tablespoon minced garlic

$\frac{1}{2}$ teaspoon freshly ground black pepper

$\frac{1}{4}$ cup extra-virgin olive oil

2 tablespoons chopped fresh basil

$\frac{1}{2}$ cup freshly grated Parmesan cheese

TOOLS

6-quart pot • measuring cups and spoons • wooden spoon • oven mitts or pot holders • colander • cutting board • chef's knife • 12-inch skillet • box grater

This dish is simple—and simply delicious! It's easy to make when you're in a hurry, so why not try it on a weeknight for your family dinner—with My Kinda Salad on page 64 and a loaf of crusty bread, you'll be set!

126

1 Bring a large pot of water to a boil over high heat.

2 Add the pasta and 1 tablespoon of the salt and return to a boil. Cook, stirring occasionally, until al dente (page 81), about 15 minutes.

3 Using oven mitts or pot holders, remove the pot of pasta from the heat and drain the pasta away from you into a colander set in the sink. Return pasta to the pot but keep off the heat.

4 While the pasta is cooking, cook the sausage in a large skillet over medium-high heat, stirring until evenly browned and cooked through, about 7 to 8 minutes.

5 Add the onion and cook, stirring, until golden brown around the edges, about 8 to 10 minutes.

6 Add the garlic, the remaining teaspoon of salt, and the pepper and cook, stirring, for 30 seconds.

7 Add the sausage mixture to the pasta. Add the olive oil and the basil, and toss to coat evenly.

8 To serve, divide equal portions of the pasta mixture among plates or soup bowls. Garnish each serving with equal portions of the Parmesan cheese.

CRUNCHY CORN CHIP PIE

YIELD: 4 to 6 servings

INGREDIENTS

1 tablespoon vegetable oil

1 pound ground beef

1½ cups chopped yellow onion

2 tablespoons minced garlic

1 tablespoon plus 1 teaspoon chili powder

1 teaspoon Baby Bam (page 25)

1 teaspoon ground cumin

1 teaspoon salt

½ teaspoon ground black pepper

1½ cups water

¼ cup tomato paste

1 teaspoon sugar

1 cup canned black beans, drained and rinsed in a colander under cool running water

4–6 cups corn chips

1 cup grated cheese such as Monterey Jack or Cheddar

1 cup chopped fresh tomato

½ cup chopped scallions

TOOLS

3½-quart saucepan • cutting board • chef's knife • measuring cups and spoons • wooden spoon • can opener • colander • box grater • oven mitts or pot holders

This is a treat for folks young and old—there's simply nothing like the crunch of crispy corn chips underneath a blanket of steaming hot chili. Top it all with some grated cheese, chopped tomatoes, and sliced scallions and you're in Tex-Mex heaven.

1 Heat the oil in a saucepan over medium heat. Add the ground beef and cook, stirring, until browned and all pink has disappeared, about 5 minutes.

2 Add the onion, garlic, chili powder, Baby Bam, cumin, salt, and black pepper. Cook, stirring, until the onions are soft, about 4 minutes.

3 Add the water, tomato paste, and sugar, and stir to mix. Bring to a boil. Reduce the heat to medium-low and cook, uncovered, until most of the liquid has evaporated, about 20 minutes.

4 Add the beans and simmer until heated through, about 2 minutes. Remove the pan from heat.

5 To serve, put one cup of corn chips in each bowl. Top with equal portions of the meat mixture.

6 Garnish each serving with some of the cheese, tomato, and scallions.

STEP 5

BREAD 'EM AND BAKE 'EM PORK CHOPS

YIELD: 6 servings

INGREDIENTS

1 (5-ounce) box plain melba toast

2 teaspoons Emeril's Italian Essence or other dry Italian seasoning

2 tablespoons plus 2 teaspoons Baby Bam (page 25)

$\frac{1}{2}$ teaspoon garlic powder

$\frac{1}{4}$ cup finely grated Parmesan cheese

$\frac{1}{4}$ cup vegetable oil

2 large eggs

6 thin center-cut pork chops (about $2\frac{1}{4}$ pounds)

TOOLS

Large rimmed baking sheet • oven-proof wire rack • aluminum foil • food processor or blender • large plastic resealable food storage bag • measuring cups and spoons • box grater • medium bowl • fork • oven mitts or pot holders

These pork chops turn out extra-crispy and golden brown because they are coated with seasoned melba toast crumbs before baking. Super-easy and super-delicious! The crumbs should be coarse, so be careful not to grind the melba toast too fine. These are awesome with mashed potatoes and Minty Green Peas (page 172).

1. Position rack in center of oven and preheat the oven to 400°F.

2. Line a large rimmed baking sheet with aluminum foil and place a wire rack on top.

3. Place the melba toast in a food processor and pulse to form coarse crumbs, about 3 pulses. Be sure to follow the safety directions on pages 6–7.

4. Transfer the crumbs to a large plastic resealable food storage bag and add the Italian Essence, 2 tablespoons of the Baby Bam, the garlic powder, Parmesan cheese, and vegetable oil. Close the bag and shake to combine.

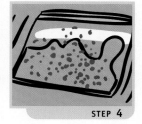

STEP 4

5. In a medium mixing bowl, beat the eggs and remaining 2 teaspoons of Baby Bam with a fork.

6. Using your hands, dip the pork chops one at a time into the eggs, then place in the bag, close, and shake to coat on both sides, pressing so that the crumbs adhere.

7. Place the chops on the wire rack on the baking sheet.

STEP 6

CAUTION You have to be sure to cook pork well. See page 24 for extra help.

8. Bake until the pork chops are cooked through and the coating is golden brown and crisp, about 20 minutes.

9. Using oven mitts or pot holders, remove the baking sheet from the oven and serve the chops immediately.

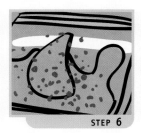

STEP 6

SHEPHERD'S PIE

YIELD: 6 servings

INGREDIENTS

5 tablespoons unsalted butter

3 large Idaho potatoes (about 2 pounds), peeled and cut into 1-inch cubes

2 teaspoons salt

$\frac{1}{2}$ cup milk

$\frac{1}{4}$ cup heavy cream

$\frac{1}{4}$ teaspoon plus $\frac{1}{8}$ teaspoon freshly ground black pepper

1 tablespoon vegetable oil

1 cup chopped yellow onion

1 teaspoon minced garlic

$1\frac{1}{2}$ pounds ground lamb or beef

$\frac{3}{4}$ teaspoon Emeril's Italian Essence or other dry Italian seasoning

$\frac{1}{4}$ teaspoon dried thyme leaves

$\frac{1}{4}$ teaspoon ground cinnamon

Pinch ground cloves

1 tablespoon all-purpose flour

$1\frac{1}{4}$ cups reduced-sodium beef broth

$\frac{3}{4}$ cup diced carrots

$\frac{1}{2}$ cup green peas, fresh or frozen (if frozen, do not thaw)

2 teaspoons tomato paste

$\frac{1}{2}$ cup grated sharp Cheddar cheese

TOOLS

2-quart casserole or soufflé dish • vegetable peeler • measuring cups and spoons • $3\frac{1}{2}$-quart saucepan • fork • oven mitts or pot holders • colander • potato masher • 10- to 12-inch skillet • wooden spoon • cutting board • chef's knife • tablespoon • bowl • can opener • box grater

This English dish is called a cottage pie if made with beef instead of lamb, but feel free to use whichever type of meat you and your family prefer. A traditional shepherd's pie has diced carrots and peas, but if you're not a big veggie fan, it's just as good without them. This dish will warm you through and through—it's ideal for a cold, wintry day.

1 Grease a casserole dish with 1 tablespoon of the butter and set aside.

2 Position rack in center of oven and preheat the oven to 375°F.

3 In a medium saucepan, place the potatoes and 1 teaspoon of the salt. Cover with water by 1 inch and bring to a boil over high heat.

4 Reduce the heat and cook at a low boil until fork-tender, about 12 to 15 minutes.

5 Using oven mitts or pot holders, drain potatoes in a colander set in the sink and then return them to the saucepan. Add the remaining 4 tablespoons of butter, the milk, heavy cream, $\frac{1}{2}$ teaspoon of the salt, and $\frac{1}{8}$ teaspoon of the black pepper. Mash with a potato masher until smooth. Set aside.

6 In a large skillet, heat the vegetable oil over medium-high heat. Add the onion and cook, stirring, until soft, about 3 minutes.

7 Add the garlic and cook, stirring, for 30 seconds, then add the ground lamb or beef and cook, stirring to break up the meat chunks, until cooked through, about 8 minutes.

8 Remove the pan from the heat. Tilt the pan slightly away from you, and with a tablespoon carefully remove as much excess liquid as possible from the pan into a bowl. Discard the liquid.

STEP 8

9 Return the skillet to medium-high heat. Add the Italian Essence, thyme, the remaining $\frac{1}{2}$ teaspoon of salt, the remaining $\frac{1}{4}$ teaspoon of black pepper, the cinnamon, and cloves, and cook until the meat is well browned, stirring frequently, about 6 to 8 minutes.

10 Sprinkle the meat with the flour and cook, stirring, for about 1 to 2 minutes.

11 Add the beef broth, carrots, peas, and tomato paste, stir to combine, and bring to a boil.

12 Reduce the heat to medium-low and simmer until thickened, about 5 to 6 minutes.

13 Transfer the mixture to the prepared casserole dish and spoon the mashed potatoes evenly over the top. Sprinkle with the cheese and bake for 30 minutes.

STEP 13

14 Increase the oven temperature to broil and cook until golden brown and crisp around the edges, about 4 to 6 minutes.

15 Using oven mitts or pot holders, remove the casserole from the oven and let it sit for 10 minutes before serving. This pan will be very hot, so be very, very careful!

JUNIOR WELLINGTONS

YIELD: 4 servings

INGREDIENTS

$1\frac{1}{2}$ pounds lean ground beef

3 egg yolks, kept in separate small containers

$\frac{1}{4}$ cup buttermilk

$4\frac{1}{2}$ teaspoons Worcestershire sauce

1 tablespoon Baby Bam (page 25)

1 tablespoon minced garlic

1 teaspoon Emeril's Italian Essence or other dry Italian seasoning

$\frac{1}{2}$ teaspoon salt

2 tablespoons all-purpose flour

2 sheets frozen puff pastry (one 17.3-ounce package), defrosted as instructed on package

1 tablespoon water

4 slices American cheese

TOOLS

Large bowl • cutting board • chef's knife • measuring cups and spoons • wooden spoon • 10-inch skillet • plate • large baking sheet • parchment paper • rolling pin • 6-inch cookie-cutter round or any 6-inch circle such as a small plate or the top of a bowl • medium bowl • whisk • pastry brush • fork • paring knife • oven mitts or pot holders

Beef Wellington is traditionally a fancy dish made by wrapping a beef tenderloin, or individual beef filets, inside puff pastry. My Junior Wellingtons add a twist to this classic *and* make it family friendly by using ground beef so that you can serve it any night of the week. You'll be surprised how quickly these can be made with everybody helping—and how much they'll impress your friends!

134

1. In a large bowl, combine the beef, 2 of the egg yolks, buttermilk, Worcestershire sauce, Baby Bam, garlic, Italian Essence, and salt. Using a wooden spoon or your clean hands, stir well to combine.

2. Divide the meat into 4 equal portions, about ¾ cup each. Pat into patties 3½ inches in diameter and 1 inch thick each. Wash your hands.

3. Heat a large skillet over medium heat and, when hot, cook 2 patties at a time until browned on both sides but not cooked all the way through: 2 minutes on the first side, and 1 minute on the second side.

4. Remove the patties from the skillet and set aside on a plate to cool. Repeat with the remaining patties. Refrigerate the patties for 30 minutes.

5. Position rack in center of oven and preheat the oven to 425°F. Line a large baking sheet with parchment paper and set aside.

6. While the meat is cooling, lightly dust a work surface with the flour. Roll out one puff pastry sheet to about ¹/₁₆-inch thickness and cut four 6-inch rounds from the sheet.

STEP 6

7. Repeat with the remaining puff pastry sheet.

8. In a medium bowl, combine the remaining egg yolk with the water and beat with a whisk or fork to make an egg wash.

STEP 9

9. Place 4 of the pastry rounds on the prepared baking sheet and, using the pastry brush, paint a ½-inch border of the egg wash around each of the 4 rounds.

10. Place a chilled hamburger patty in the middle of the round and top each with 1 slice of cheese, letting the edges hang over the sides of the patty.

STEP 10

11. Top the cheese with the remaining pastry rounds, pressing the edges together with a fork to seal.

12. Paint the top and sides of each pastry round with the egg wash and, using the tip of a paring knife, cut a small "x" in the top of each Wellington to allow steam to escape.

STEP 11

13. Bake the Wellingtons until golden brown, about 15 to 20 minutes.

14. Using oven mitts or pot holders, remove the baking sheet from the oven and serve the Wellingtons immediately.

STEP 12

CHICKEN PARMESAN EMERIL-STYLE

YIELD: 4 servings

INGREDIENTS

4 boneless skinless chicken breasts (5 to 6 ounces each)

2 teaspoons Baby Bam (page 25)

2 tablespoons olive oil

1 cup Emeril's Kicked Up Tomato Sauce, or your favorite red pasta sauce

1/4 pound mozzarella cheese, cut into 4 equal portions

1/4 cup grated Parmesan cheese

1/2 pound cooked linguine, fettuccine, or other pasta

TOOLS

Measuring cups and spoons • large ovenproof skillet (without wooden or plastic handles) • tongs • cutting board • chef's knife • box grater • oven mitts or pot holders

Talk about a classic Italian dish that everyone loves—this is it! I've made a couple of changes to make it a bit lighter than most, but I know you'll love it just the same. Round out your menu by serving this with My Kinda Salad (page 64) and some garlic bread.

1 Position rack in upper third of oven and preheat to broil (see sidebar below).

2 Season each chicken breast with ½ teaspoon (¼ teaspoon per side) of the Baby Bam.

CAUTION

Please follow the directions for handling raw poultry on page 5 very carefully!

3 Heat the olive oil in a large skillet over medium heat.

4 Put the chicken, smooth side down, in the skillet and cook for 4 minutes. Using tongs, turn the chicken breasts to the other side and cook for 2 minutes longer. Remove the skillet from the heat.

5 Pour ¼ cup of the tomato sauce over each breast.

6 Top each breast with a portion of the mozzarella cheese and one tablespoon of the Parmesan cheese.

7 Using oven mitts or pot holders, carefully place the skillet under the broiler and cook until the cheese melts, bubbles, and is lightly golden, about 2 to 3 minutes. Remember, broiler temperatures are very hot— have an adult help here.

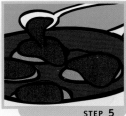

STEP 5

8 Using oven mitts or pot holders, remove the skillet from the oven. Serve the chicken over the cooked pasta of your choice.

If your broiler is separate from your oven, please have an adult show you how your broiler works.

RAINY-DAY BBQ CHICKEN

YIELD: 4 servings

INGREDIENTS

1 fryer chicken (about 3 pounds) cut into 8 pieces

3 cups apple cider

$\frac{1}{2}$ cup cider vinegar

$\frac{1}{2}$ cup Worcestershire sauce

1 tablespoon Baby Bam (page 25)

1 teaspoon salt

1 teaspoon fresh lemon juice

1 tablespoon vegetable oil

2 cups Barbecue Sauce (see recipe below or use your favorite store-bought brand)

TOOLS

Cutting board • chef's knife • large resealable plastic food storage bag • measuring cups and spoons • juicer (optional) • medium mixing bowl • whisk • 9 x 13-inch baking dish • oven mitts or pot holders • pastry brush

BARBECUE SAUCE

YIELD: 2 cups

INGREDIENTS

1$\frac{1}{2}$ cups ketchup

4 tablespoons ($\frac{1}{2}$ stick) unsalted butter

$\frac{1}{4}$ cup cider vinegar

$\frac{1}{4}$ cup packed dark brown sugar

1 tablespoon Worcestershire sauce

1 teaspoon Baby Bam (page 25)

$\frac{1}{4}$ teaspoon dry mustard

TOOLS

2- to 3-quart saucepan • measuring cups and spoons • wooden spoon • oven mitts or pot holders

Talk about good! With this chicken, you can still enjoy BBQ flavor on cold or rainy days when grilling outside is not an option. I suggest you make some extra. . . . I just know you're gonna need it!

1. Place the chicken in a resealable plastic food storage bag.

CAUTION Please follow the directions for handling raw poultry on page 5 very carefully!

2. Combine the apple cider, cider vinegar, Worcestershire sauce, Baby Bam, salt, and lemon juice in a mixing bowl and whisk to blend.

3. Pour the marinade over the chicken in the plastic storage bag, seal, and refrigerate for at least 30 minutes or for as long as 8 hours, turning occasionally to ensure even coating.

STEP 3

4. Position rack in center of oven and preheat the oven to 375°F. Grease a 9 by 13-inch baking dish with the vegetable oil and set aside.

CAUTION Be careful when broiling. It's best if an adult is in the kitchen to help—you're cooking with seriously high heat here! If your broiler is separate from your oven, have an adult show you how to use it.

5. Drain the marinade from the chicken and discard the liquid.

6. Put the chicken in the prepared baking dish. Using oven mitts or pot holders, place the dish in the oven and bake, uncovered, for 30 minutes.

7. While the chicken is baking, make the Barbecue Sauce.

8. Using oven mitts or pot holders, remove the baking dish from the oven and, using a pastry brush, coat the chicken with 1 cup of barbecue sauce. Increase the oven temperature to broil.

STEP 8

9. Using oven mitts or pot holders, return the baking dish to the oven and broil until the barbecue sauce begins to bubble and form a nice crust on the chicken, about 5 to 10 minutes.

10. Using oven mitts or pot holders, remove the baking dish from oven and allow to cool for 10 minutes before serving. Serve with the remaining barbecue sauce.

BARBECUE SAUCE

1. Combine all the ingredients in a medium saucepan over medium heat.

2. Cook, stirring occasionally, until the sauce thickens slightly, about 15 minutes.

3. Remove from heat and reserve the sauce for use with chicken.

This sauce will keep for several weeks if refrigerated in a nonreactive container.

PERFECT ROAST CHICKEN

YIELD: 4 servings

INGREDIENTS

2 medium Idaho potatoes (about 1½ pounds), peeled and cut into 1-inch wedges

3 medium carrots, peeled and cut into 1-inch pieces (about 1½ cups)

3 medium celery ribs, trimmed and cut into 1-inch pieces (about 1½ cups)

1 medium yellow onion, peeled and cut into 1-inch wedges (about 1½ cups)

¼ cup plus 1 tablespoon olive oil

2 teaspoons salt

1 teaspoon ground black pepper

1 teaspoon Baby Bam (page 25)

1 broiler chicken (about 3½ pounds), giblets and cavity fat removed, rinsed well and patted dry

3 cloves garlic, peeled

3 sprigs thyme

1 bay leaf

TOOLS

Cutting board • chef's knife • vegetable peeler • measuring cups and spoons • 2 medium bowls • large roasting pan • instant-read thermometer • oven mitts or pot holders • long tongs • carving fork and carving knife

There's nothing like the simple goodness of a perfectly roasted chicken—and now you can make it at home for your family. Just remember, it's important that you don't overcook the chicken; otherwise, the meat will be dry. Teamwork is important here—the adults will need to check for when the chicken is done. I like to serve this with the Real-Deal Rice Pilaf (page 162)—it's the perfect family meal for any day of the week, any time of the year.

1 Position rack in center of oven and preheat the oven to 500°F.

2 Place the potatoes, carrots, celery, and onion in a medium bowl and toss with ¼ cup of the olive oil, 1 teaspoon of the salt, ½ teaspoon of the black pepper, and ½ teaspoon of the Baby Bam. Spread the vegetables in an even layer along the bottom of a large roasting pan.

3 Place the chicken in a second medium bowl and rub it with the remaining 1 tablespoon of olive oil, the remaining teaspoon of salt, remaining ½ teaspoon of black pepper, and remaining ½ teaspoon of Baby Bam.

> **CAUTION** Please follow the directions for handling raw poultry on page 5 very carefully!

4 Place the garlic, thyme sprigs, and bay leaf inside the chicken cavity.

5 Place the chicken, breast side up, on top of the vegetables in the roasting pan. Wash hands well.

STEP 4

6 Roast the chicken for 20 minutes, then reduce the oven temperature to 375°F and continue to cook until the skin of the chicken is crisp and deep golden brown, and an instant-read thermometer registers 160°F when inserted into the joint of the thigh and drumstick—about 40 more minutes (page 23–24).

7 Using oven mitts or pot holders, remove the pan from the oven and let the chicken rest for 15 minutes before carving.

STEP 5

8 Using long tongs, carefully transfer the chicken to a cutting board. Have an adult help or show you how to carve the chicken into serving pieces. Serve with the vegetables and pan juices.

STEP 6

CLASSIC ROAST TURKEY

YIELD: 10 to 12 servings

INGREDIENTS

1 (10- to 12-pound) turkey

1½ teaspoons salt

¾ teaspoon ground black pepper

1 medium yellow onion, coarsely chopped

1 carrot, peeled and coarsely chopped

1 rib celery, coarsely chopped

5 sprigs fresh thyme (or ½ teaspoon dried thyme)

1 bay leaf

1 teaspoon Baby Bam (page 25)

4 tablespoons (½ stick) unsalted butter, softened at room temperature

1 cup reduced-sodium chicken broth

1 double or triple recipe of the gravy on page 86 (optional)

TOOLS

Large roasting pan with rack • paper towels • vegetable peeler • cutting board • chef's knife • measuring cups and spoons • kitchen twine • oven mitts or pot holders • can opener (optional) • baster • aluminum foil • instant-read thermometer • carving knife and fork

Now everybody can play a big part in the family's Thanksgiving dinner! Just like the Perfect Roast Chicken on page 140, this is a family classic that is a whole lot easier to make than you might think, especially with everybody pitching in. It just takes a while to cook, but hey—while the bird's roasting in the oven, make a double or triple batch of the gravy on page 86 and maybe another side dish, such as the Simple–But–Fabulous Stuffing on page 164. Then when the turkey's done, let the feast begin!

If you purchase a frozen turkey, you must defrost it in the refrigerator, and it can take several days to completely defrost, depending on the size of your bird. Make sure you read the instructions on the turkey packaging so that you allow yourself enough time before turkey day! Also, you should never try to defrost a turkey on your kitchen counter or in the kitchen sink—this promotes the growth of harmful bacteria.

1. Position rack in the lower third of oven and preheat the oven to 425°F. Fit a roasting rack inside a roasting pan.

2. Transfer the turkey to the kitchen sink and remove its wrapping. Using your hands, remove and discard the neck, gizzards, heart, and liver usually found in a small paper or plastic bag inside the cavity.

3. Rinse the turkey well inside and out under cold running water. Pat dry inside and out with paper towels and transfer the turkey breast side up to the rack in the roasting pan.

CAUTION Please follow the directions for handling raw poultry on page 5 very carefully!

4. Season the inside of the turkey with ½ teaspoon of the salt and ½ teaspoon of the black pepper and stuff the cavity of the turkey with the onion, carrots, celery, thyme sprigs, and bay leaf.

STEP 5

5. Using kitchen twine, tie the ends of the turkey's legs together so that it looks as if it is trying to cross its legs.

(continued)

6 Season the outside of the turkey evenly with the remaining 1 teaspoon of salt, ¼ teaspoon black pepper, and the Baby Bam.

7 Use your hands to rub the butter evenly over the entire turkey. You might have to ask someone to hold the turkey for you while you do this. Wash hands well.

8 Transfer the turkey to the oven and bake, uncovered, for 30 minutes.

9 Reduce the oven temperature to 350°F and, with oven mitts or pot holders, carefully remove the roasting pan from the oven. Watch it, this is heavy and now it's hot too!

10 Using a baster, baste the top of the turkey evenly with ⅓ of the chicken broth (page 21).

STEP 10

11 Using oven mitts or pot holders, return the turkey to the oven and cook for an additional 1¾ to 2 hours, basting twice more during this cooking time with the remaining chicken broth. Always use oven mitts or pot holders for handling the hot roasting pan. If the turkey begins to look too browned, cover the top loosely with aluminum foil until it is done.

To be sure that your bird is completely cooked, insert an instant-read thermometer deeply into the joint of the leg and thigh without touching the thigh bone. When the thermometer measures 165°F, your bird is ready to be removed from the oven.

12 After 1¾ to 2 hours, the turkey should be a nice golden brown color, and the juices should run clear when you insert the tip of a knife at the joint of the leg and thigh.

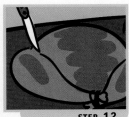

STEP 12

13 Using oven mitts or pot holders, carefully remove the roasting pan from the oven and cover the turkey loosely with aluminum foil. Let the turkey sit for about 20 to 30 minutes before carving. Save the drippings in the pan if you plan to make gravy (see page 86 and sidebar below).

14 Have an experienced adult help you transfer the turkey to a carving board and show you how to carve the turkey—then serve.

If I were you, I'd make a double or triple batch of the gravy on page 86 to go with my turkey, then I'd kick it up like real home cooks do by adding the turkey drippings from the roasting pan. To do this, you'll first have to "defat" the drippings: Once you've transferred the turkey to a carving board, use oven mitts or pot holders to carefully tilt the roasting pan away from you. Have an adult help you skim a spoon over the very top of the liquid so that only the fat is skimmed off and the tasty drippings are left behind. Discard the fat skimmings. Transfer the drippings to the saucepan with the prepared gravy, and then simmer a bit until the gravy is thickened and flavorful.

FISH IN A POUCH

YIELD: 4 servings

INGREDIENTS

8 tablespoons (1 stick) unsalted butter, softened at room temperature

2 teaspoons Worcestershire sauce

1 tablespoon chopped fresh parsley

1 teaspoon minced garlic

$\frac{1}{8}$ teaspoon salt

$\frac{1}{8}$ teaspoon ground white pepper

4 (8-ounce) white fish fillets such as flounder, sole, cod, scrod, or whitefish

2 teaspoons Baby Bam (page 25)

TOOLS

Small mixing bowl • measuring spoons • cutting board • chef's knife • rubber spatula • 4 sheets of aluminum foil, 12 x 8 inches each • baking sheet • oven mitts or pot holders • kitchen scissors (optional)

This dish is inspired by the classic French preparation called *en papillote*, in which food is baked inside a pouch of parchment paper. To make it easier, I've used aluminum foil to wrap fish topped with compound butter. What's compound butter, you say? Oh, not to worry—that's just a fancy term for butter creamed with other ingredients for added flavor. Here it makes our fish super-moist and delicious.

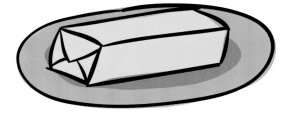

146

1. In a small mixing bowl, combine the butter, Worcestershire sauce, parsley, garlic, salt, and white pepper. Use a rubber spatula to mix the ingredients well until smooth. This is called a compound butter.

STEP 5

2. Position rack in center of oven and preheat the oven to 375°F.

3. Season each fish fillet with ½ teaspoon of the Baby Bam.

4. Lay each fillet in the center of a piece of aluminum foil and spoon 2 tablespoons of the compound butter over the top of the fish.

5. Bring the long edges of the aluminum foil together and make thin folds to form an airtight seal. One side at a time, bring the outer short edges together and fold two or three times inward to seal the sides of the pouch.

STEP 5

6. Repeat with the remaining fish fillets.

7. Lay the pouches on a baking sheet and place in the oven.

8. Bake for 20 minutes.

9. Using oven mitts or pot holders, remove the baking sheet from the oven and cut the pouches open with kitchen scissors, or carefully unfold the pouches. Watch out for steam—keep your face away!

STEP 5

10. Serve immediately.

EMERIL'S FAVORITE STUFFED SHRIMP

YIELD: 20 stuffed shrimp, serving 4 as an entrée or 8 as an appetizer

INGREDIENTS

5 tablespoons unsalted butter

1 pound fresh lump crabmeat, picked over for shells and cartilage

2¼ teaspoons Baby Bam (page 25)

½ cup minced yellow onion

¼ cup minced celery

¼ cup minced green bell pepper

¼ cup plus 1 tablespoon finely chopped fresh parsley

1 tablespoon minced garlic

¼ cup mayonnaise

1 egg, lightly beaten

3 tablespoons fresh lemon juice

1 tablespoon Worcestershire sauce

1½ teaspoons Emeril's Hot Sauce or other red hot sauce

1½ cups crushed Ritz crackers

½ teaspoon salt

¼ teaspoon freshly ground black pepper

20 fresh jumbo shrimp (about 2 pounds), peeled, leaving tail and first connecting shell segment, deveined, and butterflied lengthwise (page 17)

3 tablespoons melted unsalted butter for drizzling over the shrimp

1 lemon, cut into wedges

TOOLS

Measuring cups and spoons • small saucepan • large baking dish • large mixing bowl • plastic wrap • 8-inch skillet • cutting board • chef's knife • small bowl • fork • juicer (optional) • wooden spoon • paring knife • oven mitts or pot holders

This is one of my all-time favorite dishes from childhood, and everybody can help make these tender, plump shrimp. They're filled with crabmeat stuffing, topped with crumbled Ritz crackers, and drizzled with butter. Oh baby, you're playing with my emotions!

1. Position rack in center of oven and preheat the oven to 375°F. Using 1 tablespoon of the butter, grease a large baking dish and set aside.

2. Place the crabmeat in a large bowl and season with 2 teaspoons of the Baby Bam. Cover with plastic wrap and refrigerate until ready to use.

3. In a medium skillet, melt the remaining 4 tablespoons of the butter over medium-high heat. Add the onion, celery, and bell pepper and cook, stirring, until softened, about 4 minutes. Add ¼ cup of the parsley and the garlic, and cook, stirring, for 1 minute. Remove from heat and let cool.

4. Add the cooled vegetables to the crabmeat and toss to combine. Add the mayonnaise, beaten egg, lemon juice, Worcestershire sauce, and hot sauce and stir gently with a large wooden spoon. Add 1 cup of the cracker crumbs, the salt, and pepper, and stir gently, being careful not to break up the crabmeat.

5. Season the peeled, deveined shrimp lightly with the remaining ¼ teaspoon of the Baby Bam. Mound about 2 tablespoons of the crabmeat stuffing onto the top of each shrimp, pressing gently so that stuffing sticks to shrimp.

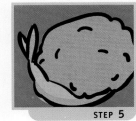

STEP 5

6. Place the shrimp, stuffed sides up, in the prepared baking dish and sprinkle the remaining ½ cup of the cracker crumbs over the tops of the shrimp. Drizzle with the melted butter. Using oven mitts or pot holders, place the baking dish in the oven and bake until golden, about 25 minutes.

STEP 6

7. Using oven mitts or pot holders, remove the baking dish from the oven and divide the shrimp among plates. Garnish with the remaining tablespoon of parsley and the lemon wedges. Serve immediately.

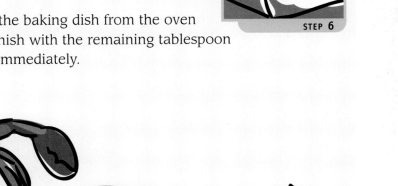

MAMBO RICE "LASAGNA"

YIELD: 12 to 16 servings

INGREDIENTS

1 boneless pork shoulder roast, such as Boston butt or picnic (about 6 pounds)

Juice of 3 limes, or 1/2 cup lime juice

Juice of 1 1/2 oranges, or 1/2 cup orange juice

2 tablespoons crushed dried oregano

1 teaspoon ground cumin

12 cloves garlic, minced (about 6 tablespoons minced)

2 tablespoons salt

2 (15-ounce) cans black beans, undrained

2 tablespoons plus 1/4 cup vegetable oil

2 cups water

2 cups long-grain white rice

1 3/4 teaspoons ground black pepper

6 very ripe plantains (outside skin must be black)

1/2 cup olive oil

1 pint cherry tomatoes, washed and halved or quartered

1/3 cup finely chopped fresh parsley or cilantro

TOOLS

Large resealable plastic food storage bag • small bowl • juicer (optional) • measuring cups and spoons • cutting board • chef's knife • whisk • large roasting pan with rack • aluminum foil • oven mitts or pot holders • 2 forks • medium bowl • 3 1/2- to 4-quart saucepan with a lid • can opener • wooden spoon • large skillet • tongs • paper towel–lined plates • small saucepan or skillet • large deep lasagna or roasting pan, about 10 x 15 inches

My friend Julio Yanes won the HarperCollins EMERIL'S THERE'S A CHEF IN MY SOUP! recipe contest with this awesome recipe. He was inspired by his grandmother Tessie's rice and beans, Cuban-style roast pork, and fried sweet plantains. He combined these three already fabulous dishes together to make one extremely kicked-up "lasagna," and then came up with a garlic oil to drizzle all over the top of everything. Oh, Julio, you really knocked our socks off with this one! Thanks to Julio, I'm happy to share this recipe with all of you. Though it seems difficult to make, it's just many simple steps put together, but you need to start the day before and read the whole recipe through first. Good things sometimes take time!

DAY 1:

1. Place the pork in a large resealable plastic food storage bag and set aside.

2. In a bowl, combine the lime juice, orange juice, oregano, cumin, and 3 tablespoons of the minced garlic and whisk to combine thoroughly.

3. Pour the juice mixture over the pork and seal the storage bag. Place in the refrigerator to marinate overnight, turning occasionally.

DAY 2:

4. The next morning, remove the pork from the refrigerator and allow it to return to room temperature while still in the bag before proceeding.

5. Position rack in center of oven and preheat the oven to 350°F. Line a roasting pan with aluminum foil and place a roasting rack inside the roasting pan.

6. Remove the pork from the marinade and discard the marinade. Season the pork with 1 tablespoon of the salt and the pepper.

7. Place the pork on the rack, fat side up. Cover with aluminum foil and bake for 4 hours. Start preparing the rice and beans and plantains (page 152).

8. Using oven mitts or pot holders, remove the foil from the roast and continue to bake until roast is very tender and pulls apart easily with a fork, about 2 hours longer.

9. Using oven mitts or pot holders, remove the pork from the oven and set aside to cool.

10. When the pork is cool enough to handle, remove any excess fat from the meat with a fork and discard. Using two forks or your clean hands, shred the pork into bite-size pieces. Set aside in a medium clean bowl.

STEP 10

(continued)

1. While the pork is roasting, in a medium saucepan combine the canned, undrained black beans, 2 tablespoons of the vegetable oil, 2 teaspoons of the salt, and the water and bring to a boil over high heat.

2. Using a wooden spoon, stir in the rice and return to a boil. Cover the pan with a tight-fitting lid and reduce the heat to medium-low so that the rice just simmers. Cook until the rice is tender and has absorbed the cooking liquid, about 20 to 25 minutes.

STEP 3

3. Meanwhile, to peel the plantains—which do not peel like regular bananas, top to bottom—carefully run a sharp knife down the length of the plantain in several spots. Then you can simply peel away the skin by opening it side to side.

4. Slice the peeled plantains crosswise on a diagonal into $\frac{1}{2}$-inch-thick slices.

STEP 4

5. In a large skillet, heat the remaining $\frac{1}{4}$ cup of vegetable oil over medium-high heat and sauté the plantain slices, in batches if necessary, until golden brown on both sides, turning with tongs to ensure even browning, about $1\frac{1}{2}$ to 2 minutes on each side. Transfer to plates lined with paper towels to drain briefly, then set plantains aside until ready to assemble the casserole.

STEP 5

6. In a small saucepan or skillet, heat the $\frac{1}{2}$ cup olive oil over low heat and add the remaining 3 tablespoons of minced garlic. Cook slowly until the garlic is softened and very aromatic but not browned, about 4 to 5 minutes. Set aside to cool.

ASSEMBLING THE "LASAGNA":

1. Position rack in center of oven and preheat the oven to 350°F.

2. When all of the elements are ready, spread half of the rice and bean mixture evenly along the bottom of a lasagna pan.

3. Top with the shredded pork, and season with ½ teaspoon salt. Top this with the fried plantains and season with the remaining ½ teaspoon of salt.

4. Place the remaining rice and bean mixture over the plantains and drizzle the reserved garlic oil mixture over the top. Cover with aluminum foil.

5. Using oven mitts or pot holders, place the "lasagna" in the oven until heated through, about 30 minutes.

6. Using oven mitts or pot holders, remove the "lasagna" from the oven and serve garnished with the cherry tomatoes and parsley.

STEP 2

STEP 3

STEP 4

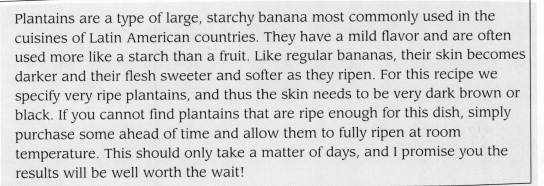

Plantains are a type of large, starchy banana most commonly used in the cuisines of Latin American countries. They have a mild flavor and are often used more like a starch than a fruit. Like regular bananas, their skin becomes darker and their flesh sweeter and softer as they ripen. For this recipe we specify very ripe plantains, and thus the skin needs to be very dark brown or black. If you cannot find plantains that are ripe enough for this dish, simply purchase some ahead of time and allow them to fully ripen at room temperature. This should only take a matter of days, and I promise you the results will be well worth the wait!

Sides that Sizzle

OVEN-ROASTED VEGGIES

YIELD: 6 servings

INGREDIENTS

3 tablespoons extra-virgin olive oil

2 teaspoons salt

1 teaspoon Emeril's Italian Essence or other dry Italian seasoning

$\frac{1}{2}$ teaspoon freshly ground black pepper

$\frac{1}{2}$ teaspoon Baby Bam (page 25)

1 pound red potatoes, cut into eighths or bite-size pieces

1 pound carrots (about 3 cups, or 6 medium carrots), peeled and sliced into 1-inch pieces

1 medium yellow onion (about 1$\frac{1}{2}$ cups), chopped into eighths or bite-size pieces

1 medium yellow squash (about 1$\frac{1}{2}$ cups), chopped into 1-inch pieces

1 medium red bell pepper (about 1 cup), chopped into 1-inch pieces

TOOLS

Measuring cups and spoons • 2 medium bowls • vegetable peeler • cutting board • chef's knife • roasting pan, preferably nonstick • oven mitts or pot holders • wooden spoon

This is a crowd-pleasing dish you can make for almost any family meal. With so many veggies to choose from, there will be something in this dish for everyone to like. And they really rock when paired with the Fish in a Pouch on page 146. Kick it up with some garlic or add some chopped fresh rosemary and thyme. Fresh herbs rule!

156

1   Position rack in center of oven and preheat the oven to 425°F.

2   Combine 1 tablespoon of the olive oil, 1 teaspoon of the salt, $\frac{1}{2}$ teaspoon of the Italian Essence, $\frac{1}{4}$ teaspoon of the black pepper, and $\frac{1}{4}$ teaspoon of the Baby Bam in a medium bowl.

3   Toss the potatoes in this mixture and place them in a roasting pan. Using oven mitts or pot holders, transfer the pan to the oven and roast for 20 minutes.

4   Meanwhile, combine the remaining 2 tablespoons of olive oil, 1 teaspoon salt, $\frac{1}{2}$ teaspoon Italian Essence, $\frac{1}{4}$ teaspoon black pepper, and $\frac{1}{4}$ teaspoon Baby Bam in another medium bowl. Toss the carrots, onion, squash, and bell pepper in this mixture and reserve for roasting.

5   After the initial 20-minute roasting of potatoes, remove the pan from the oven using oven mitts or pot holders. Add the carrots, onion, squash, and bell pepper to the potatoes and, using a wooden spoon, stir to combine.

6   Using oven mitts or pot holders, return the roasting pan to the oven and increase the temperature to 475°F. Roast until all the vegetables are tender and have a nice color, about 40 minutes longer. (Stir the pan at least once during cooking to ensure even browning of the vegetables.)

7   Using oven mitts or pot holders, remove the pan from the oven, allow to cool for 10 minutes, and serve.

> If using a nonstick pan, there is no need to coat it with olive oil or stir the roasting vegetables too frequently. However, if using a regular pan you will need to coat the pan with about 2 tablespoons of olive oil before roasting the vegetables, and you will need to stir your roasting vegetables more frequently (about every 20 minutes).

CORN-OFF-THE-COB PUDDING

YIELD: 6 servings

INGREDIENTS

1½ teaspoons unsalted butter

3 quarts water

⅓ cup honey

6 ears fresh corn, husked and silk removed

3 large eggs

1 cup heavy cream

½ cup milk

½ teaspoon ground white pepper

½ teaspoon salt

¼ teaspoon nutmeg

⅛ teaspoon cayenne pepper (optional)

¼ cup grated yellow onion

TOOLS

8-inch casserole or 2-quart soufflé dish • measuring cups and spoons • 6-quart pot • tongs • medium mixing bowl • large mixing bowl • whisk • cutting board • chef's knife • wooden spoon • box grater • oven mitts or pot holders

This traditional Southern side dish makes a wonderful addition to a holiday menu. It goes with any type of pork but is especially at home next to baked ham. You can cook it in either a casserole or a soufflé dish—but keep in mind that a deep dish will need to cook a little longer than a shallow dish. The secret to the intense corn flavor is adding a little honey to wake up the sweetness in the corn. Mmmm.

1 Position rack in center of oven and preheat the oven to 350°F.

2 Butter a casserole or soufflé dish with the butter and set aside.

3 In a large pot, bring the water and honey to a boil over high heat. Add the corn and cook for 3 minutes. Remove the pot from the heat.

4 With tongs, carefully remove the corn from the water and transfer to a medium bowl. Let sit until cool enough to handle, about 5 minutes.

5 In a large bowl, whisk together the eggs, cream, milk, white pepper, salt, nutmeg, and cayenne pepper, if desired.

6 One at a time, hold the corn in one hand and stand it on the thicker end so that it is "standing up" on the cutting board.

> **CAUTION** An adult should really do this next step since it's very tricky and you're using a large, sharp knife.

7 Hold a large chef's knife in the other hand and with a downward motion, cut the kernels from the cob. Turn the cob with every cut so that you get all of the kernels. To get even more goodness, you can also scrape the corn cobs with the back side of the chef's knife or with a spoon—this will release some of the milk from the corn. Add any juices to the cut kernels. Discard the cobs.

STEP 7

8 Add the corn kernels and onion to the egg mixture, stirring well to combine, and pour into the prepared baking dish.

9 Bake until firm in the center and golden brown on top, about 40 to 50 minutes.

10 Using oven mitts or pot holders, remove the baking dish from the oven and let it sit for 10 minutes before serving. This is best if served hot.

BEAN TOWN BAKED BEANS

YIELD: About 4 cups, serving 4 to 6

INGREDIENTS

½ pound dried navy or Great Northern beans, picked over (page 14) and soaked overnight in cold water

¼ pound bacon (4 or 5 slices), cut into ½-inch pieces

1 cup chopped yellow onion

2 teaspoons minced garlic

¾ cup dark brown sugar

1 cup ketchup

3 tablespoons maple syrup

3 tablespoons molasses

1 tablespoon Worcestershire sauce

2 teaspoons Dijon mustard

½ teaspoon salt

¼ teaspoon ground black pepper

TOOLS

Can opener (optional) • colander • 3½- to 4-quart saucepan • measuring cups and spoons • 8-inch skillet • cutting board • chef's knife • medium mixing bowl • oven mitts or pot holders • medium ovenproof saucepan with tight-fitting lid or casserole dish and aluminum foil • wooden spoon

In New England, where I grew up, folks are just crazy for baked beans. Most folks have a special pot for cooking them and their very own recipe that's been in the family for years. Boston is even affectionately nicknamed Bean Town because folks there love their baked beans so much. Try my version here—the beans are cooked long and slow just like they do in New England—for a taste of the real thing!

1. Drain the soaked beans in a colander and discard the soaking water. Transfer the beans to a medium saucepan, add 6 cups of fresh water, and bring to a boil over high heat.

2. Reduce the heat to a simmer and cook until the beans are tender, about 45 minutes to 1 hour. Set the beans aside to cool in the cooking liquid.

3. Position rack in center of the oven and preheat the oven to 300°F.

4. In a medium skillet over medium-high heat, sauté the bacon until crisp and golden brown, about 5 to 6 minutes. Be careful of grease splatters.

5. Add the onion and cook, stirring, until soft, about 4 to 5 minutes.

6. Add the garlic and cook for 2 minutes.

7. Add the brown sugar and cook, stirring, until melted, about 2 to 3 minutes.

8. Add the ketchup, maple syrup, molasses, Worcestershire sauce, Dijon mustard, salt, and pepper and stir to combine well.

9. Set a colander over a mixing bowl in the sink and, using oven mitts or pot holders, drain the cooked beans away from you, reserving the cooking liquid in the bowl.

10. Transfer the beans to an ovenproof saucepan or casserole dish. Add the bacon-ketchup mixture and stir to combine well. Cover the saucepan with the lid or aluminum foil and, using oven mitts or pot holders, transfer to the oven.

11. Bake the beans, stirring occasionally, for $2\frac{1}{2}$ hours.

12. Using oven mitts or pot holders, remove the casserole, add $\frac{1}{2}$ cup of the reserved cooking liquid, and stir. With oven mitts or pot holders, return the casserole to the oven and bake, uncovered, for 30 to 45 minutes more, stirring occasionally, until the sauce is thick and bubbly around the edges.

13. Using oven mitts or pot holders, remove the beans from the oven and serve.

> If you prefer to use canned beans, you can skip steps 1 and 2. Simply substitute 3 cups of canned cannellini, Great Northern, or navy beans, drained and rinsed, and substitute an equal amount of water for the bean cooking liquid in step 12.

REAL-DEAL RICE PILAF

YIELD: 4½ cups, serving 6

INGREDIENTS

2 tablespoons unsalted butter

½ cup chopped yellow onion

1 cup long-grain white rice

1 cup water

1 cup reduced-sodium chicken broth

1 teaspoon salt

2 tablespoons thinly sliced scallions (optional)

TOOLS

2- to 3-quart ovenproof saucepan with a tight-fitting lid • measuring cups and spoons • cutting board • chef's knife • wooden spoon • oven mitts or pot holders • fork • can opener (optional)

This dish has a wonderful, rich flavor that comes from sautéing the uncooked rice in butter *before* adding the cooking liquid. The rice is then finished in the oven, leaving your stovetop free for other things. If you want to add other flavors, go right ahead. Toasted nuts, raisins or other dried fruits, sautéed mushrooms, fresh green peas, chopped fresh herbs—any of these would make great additions to this pilaf. Let your family pick their favorites.

1 Position rack in center of oven and preheat the oven to 350°F.

2 In a medium saucepan, melt the butter over medium heat. Add the onion and cook, stirring, until soft, about 3 to 4 minutes.

3 Add the rice and cook, stirring, until opaque (cloudy), and nutty in aroma, about 2 minutes.

4 Add the water, chicken broth, and salt and bring to a boil.

5 Cover the pan with a tight-fitting lid. Using oven mitts or pot holders, transfer to the oven, and bake until the rice is tender and the liquid is absorbed, about 25 to 30 minutes.

6 Using oven mitts or pot holders, remove the pan from the oven and let sit, undisturbed, for 5 to 10 minutes.

7 Fluff the rice with a fork and stir in the scallions, if desired. Serve hot.

STEP 7

SIMPLE-BUT-FABULOUS STUFFING

YIELD: 10 to 12 servings

INGREDIENTS

¼ pound bacon (4 or 5 slices), cut into ½-inch pieces

8 tablespoons (1 stick) unsalted butter

2 cups chopped yellow onion

1 cup chopped celery

1 tablespoon plus ½ teaspoon poultry seasoning

2 teaspoons minced garlic

12 to 14 cups cubed (½-inch) day-old French bread

2 cups reduced-sodium chicken broth

2 large eggs, lightly beaten

½ cup chopped fresh parsley

2 tablespoons finely chopped scallions

½ teaspoon salt

¼ teaspoon ground black pepper

¼ teaspoon Baby Bam (page 25)

TOOLS

Cutting board • chef's knife • 10-inch skillet • tongs (optional) • small bowl • fork • wooden spoon • measuring cups and spoons • large mixing bowl • can opener (optional) • 9 x 13-inch baking dish • aluminum foil • oven mitts or pot holders

This is the perfect dish to make when you've invited a crowd for dinner, as it serves 10 to 12 people. Hey, the more the merrier, and everybody in the family can help! I like to make this along with a double or even triple batch of the gravy from page 86 to go with the Classic Roast Turkey (page 142). Add whatever veggies you like and you've got a complete holiday meal to enjoy with friends and family!

164

CAUTION

1. Position rack in center of oven and preheat the oven to 400°F.

2. Heat a medium skillet over medium-high heat and add the bacon. Cook, stirring frequently, until bacon is crisp and golden brown, about 4 to 5 minutes.

3. Add 4 tablespoons of the butter and the onion and celery to the pan with the bacon and cook until the vegetables are soft, about 5 to 6 minutes.

4. Add the poultry seasoning and garlic and cook for 2 more minutes.

5. Transfer the mixture to a large mixing bowl and add the bread cubes, chicken broth, beaten eggs, parsley, scallions, salt, pepper, and Baby Bam. Using a wooden spoon, stir to thoroughly combine. Reserve the skillet for later use.

6. Using 1 tablespoon of the remaining butter, coat the sides and bottom of a baking dish and transfer the bread mixture to the buttered baking dish.

7. In the same skillet in which you cooked the bacon, melt the remaining 3 tablespoons of butter over medium heat.

8. Carefully drizzle the melted butter over the top of the bread mixture in the baking dish.

9. Cover the baking dish with aluminum foil and bake for 30 minutes.

10. Using oven mitts or pot holders, carefully remove the baking dish from the oven and remove the aluminum foil. Be very careful of steam!

11. Using oven mitts or pot holders, return the baking dish to the oven and continue to bake until top of stuffing is golden brown and slightly crispy, about 20 minutes longer.

12. Using oven mitts or pot holders, remove the baking dish from the oven and serve.

SUGAR-AND-SPICE ACORN SQUASH

YIELD: 8 servings

INGREDIENTS

2 acorn squash (about 1½ pounds each)

6 tablespoons unsalted butter, softened at room temperature

3 tablespoons maple syrup

3 tablespoons light brown sugar

¾ teaspoon ground cinnamon

½ teaspoon ground allspice

Pinch ground cloves

Pinch grated nutmeg

¼ teaspoon plus a pinch salt

¼ teaspoon freshly ground black pepper

TOOLS

Cutting board • chef's knife • spoon • 9 x 13-inch baking dish • small mixing bowl • measuring spoons • small rubber spatula • aluminum foil • oven mitts or pot holders • fork • pastry brush • slotted spoon

I love squash—of any kind! But in the chilly fall and winter months, acorn squash baked with butter, maple syrup, brown sugar, and spices is one of my favorite side dishes. It's a colorful and yummy addition to any holiday table and your family will love it. If you can't find acorn squash, butternut squash will work just as well. Hey, you adults out there—you really need to help with this dish because the hard squash is tough to cut.

1. Position rack in center of oven and preheat the oven to 375°F.

2. On a cutting board, cut the squash in half lengthwise. An adult may have to do this, since the squash is both very hard and round. *Be very careful!*

STEP 2

3. Scrape the seeds and fibers from the squash with a spoon.

4. Cut each squash half in two and place the quarters in a baking dish so that they fit in one layer, skin side down.

5. In a small mixing bowl, combine the butter, maple syrup, brown sugar, cinnamon, allspice, cloves, nutmeg, and a pinch of salt. Mix until smooth with a rubber spatula.

STEP 3

6. Divide the butter mixture among the squash quarters, about 1 tablespoon each. Season the squash evenly with the remaining $1/4$ teaspoon of salt and the black pepper. Butter mixture will melt inside the scooped-out squash wells.

7. Cover the baking dish tightly with aluminum foil. Bake, covered, until the squash can be easily pierced with a fork, about 45 minutes.

8. Using oven mitts or pot holders, remove the baking dish from the oven and carefully remove the foil. Watch out for steam!

STEP 4

9. With the pastry brush, brush the melted butter from the squash wells evenly over the inside of each squash.

10. With oven mitts or pot holders, return the baking dish to the oven and bake, uncovered, for 20 to 30 minutes, or until the squash is golden brown around the edges.

11. Using oven mitts or pot holders, remove the dish from the oven.

STEP 9

12. Using a slotted spoon, carefully transfer the squash to serving plates and serve immediately.

> If you are a fan of toasted pumpkin seeds, I suggest you save the squash seeds and toast them in the oven for a delicious snack! Simply toss them in a bowl with a little olive oil or vegetable oil, season them with salt to taste, then spread them in an even layer on a baking sheet and bake in a moderate oven (325°-350°F) until crispy—delicious!

SIMPLY DELICIOUS ARTICHOKES

YIELD: 4 artichokes, serving 4

INGREDIENTS

4 artichokes

¼ cup plus 1 teaspoon salt

1 lemon, halved, plus 2 tablespoons lemon juice

12 tablespoons (1½ sticks) unsalted butter

TOOLS

8-quart pot • measuring cups and spoons • cutting board • chef's knife • kitchen scissors • juicer (optional) • slotted spoon or skimmer • pot lid or baking dish to fit inside the 8-quart pot • small bowl • colander • tongs • small saucepan • wooden spoon • oven mitts or pot holders

If you ask me, artichokes are one of the most overlooked vegetables. Not only are they super-delicious, but they're fun to eat and easy to prepare . . . what could be better than that? Make these for your next family dinner party! I suggest serving them with melted butter, but they're also great with mayonnaise that's been jazzed up with some Baby Bam (page 25) and a squeeze of lemon juice. Yum!

1. In a large pot, bring 3 quarts of water and ¼ cup of the salt to a boil.

2. Place the artichokes on a cutting board. With a sharp chef's knife, trim the stem ends off until the bottom is flat. This way, the artichokes can sit upright. Cut the top third from each artichoke and discard.

STEP 2

3. With kitchen scissors, cut the pointed tip from each of the remaining outer leaves. Discard.

4. Rub the cut areas with the lemon halves.

5. Squeeze any remaining juice from the lemon halves and add the juice to the boiling water along with the juiced lemon halves themselves.

STEP 3

6. Using a slotted spoon or skimmer, carefully add the artichokes to the boiling water. Top with a heavy pot lid or heat-proof baking dish that will fit inside the pot, so that the weight will keep the artichokes submerged in the water. This is a bit tricky. Be sure to have an adult help with this.

7. Lower the heat and cook at a slow boil until the artichokes are tender, about 20 to 30 minutes. With oven mitts or pot holders, carefully remove the lid or weighted dish from the top of the artichokes.

STEP 4

8. With a slotted spoon or skimmer, and with a small bowl or dish held underneath to catch the hot water, carefully transfer the artichokes to a colander set in a sink. With tongs, turn each artichoke upside down and place in the colander. Let drain, inverted, until cool enough to handle.

9. To make the lemon-butter sauce, melt the butter over medium heat in a small saucepan.

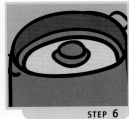

STEP 6

10. Add the remaining 2 tablespoons of lemon juice and the remaining teaspoon of salt, and stir to combine.

11. Remove the lemon-butter sauce from the heat and transfer to small dipping bowls to serve with the artichokes.

12. Serve the artichokes either warm or cold.

STEP 8

BEST BAKED TOMATOES

YIELD: 6 servings

INGREDIENTS

1 teaspoon vegetable oil

6 medium tomatoes, about 2 pounds

½ cup fine dry bread crumbs

3 tablespoons extra-virgin olive oil

2 tablespoons finely grated Parmesan cheese

1 tablespoon Baby Bam (page 25)

1 teaspoon minced garlic

TOOLS

9-inch round shallow baking dish • measuring cups and spoons • cutting board • serrated knife • 2 small mixing bowls • box grater • spoon • oven mitts or pot holders

Tomatoes are not just for salads. Here's a way to make them that will surprise your whole family—the tomato ends up soft and creamy on the inside, with a crispy layer of bread crumbs on top. If you're in the mood, you can kick them up with more garlic or add some chopped fresh basil or parsley. And hey, a little extra Parmesan cheese never hurt anyone!

170

1. Position rack in center of oven and preheat the oven to 375°F.

2. Lightly grease a 9-inch round baking dish with the vegetable oil and set aside.

3. Place the tomatoes on a cutting board and, with a serrated knife, cut the top third from each tomato. Discard the top.

4. Place each tomato over a bowl and gently squeeze to expel the seeds and pulp. Discard seeds and pulp.

STEP 4

5. Place the tomatoes in the prepared baking dish, cut side up.

6. In a small mixing bowl, combine the bread crumbs, 2 tablespoons of the olive oil, the Parmesan cheese, Baby Bam, and garlic.

7. Divide the bread crumb mixture among the 6 cut tomatoes (about 2 tablespoons each), gently packing down with the back of a spoon.

8. Drizzle the remaining 1 tablespoon olive oil evenly over the tomatoes.

9. Bake, uncovered, until the topping mixture is golden brown and the tomatoes are tender, about 30 minutes.

STEP 7

10. Using oven mitts or pot holders, remove the baking dish from the oven and let sit for 10 minutes before serving the tomatoes hot.

MINTY GREEN PEAS

YIELD: About 3 cups, serving 4 to 6

INGREDIENTS

2 tablespoons unsalted butter

1/4 cup minced yellow onion

1 pound frozen green peas, not thawed

1/2 cup water

1/2 teaspoon salt

1 tablespoon finely chopped fresh mint

TOOLS

2- to 3-quart saucepan with a lid • measuring cups and spoons • wooden spoon • cutting board • chef's knife • large slotted spoon • oven mitts or pot holders

This is a classic flavor combo that you've just got to try! Kicked up with a little onion and rolling around in some butter—green peas never had it so good! Kids, this is pretty easy to make, so this is one you can do while your folks are making another dish to go with it, such as Mighty Meaty Meatloaf (page 124) or Bread 'Em and Bake 'Em Pork Chops (page 130).

1 Melt the butter in a medium saucepan over medium-high heat.

2 Add the onion and cook, stirring, until soft, about 3 minutes.

3 Add the peas and water and bring to a boil.

4 Reduce the heat to medium-low, cover the saucepan, and simmer until tender, about 4 minutes.

5 Remove from the heat.

6 Add the salt and mint and stir.

7 Using a slotted spoon, transfer the peas to serving plates.

8 Serve hot.

Sweet Endings

CHAPTER 8

MEGAN'S WHITE CHOCOLATE BARK WITH PECANS

YIELD: Thirty-six 2 x 1½-inch pieces, serving 18 to 20 (lots!)

INGREDIENTS

1 teaspoon unsalted butter, softened at room temperature

1½ pounds white chocolate, chopped

1½ cups chopped pecans, lightly toasted (page 22)

12 ounces semisweet chocolate, chopped or morsels

TOOLS

9 x 13-inch low-rimmed baking sheet or casserole dish • measuring cups and spoons • double boiler or 2 metal bowls that fit inside a medium saucepan for melting chocolate • oven mitts or pot holders • cutting board • chef's knife • rubber spatula • dull knife or teaspoon

My friend Megan likes to make this yummy bark for her family. Her little sister, Lauren, is especially appreciative! But be forewarned—this recipe makes a whole lot of bark! Why not whip up a batch for your next big family get-together?

1 Grease a 9 by 13-inch low-rimmed baking sheet or casserole dish with the butter and set aside.

2 In the top of a double boiler or in a metal mixing bowl set over a pot of simmering water, melt the white chocolate, stirring occasionally with a rubber spatula (page 22). Use oven mitts or pot holders since the steam can burn.

> White chocolate chunks or bars work best for this recipe. We find that white chocolate morsels sometimes "seize" (clump up) when melted, so we don't recommend using them in any recipe calling for melted white chocolate.

STEP 4

3 Add the chopped toasted pecans and stir well.

4 Pour the melted white chocolate mixture into the buttered baking sheet and smooth the top with the rubber spatula.

5 Clean out the top of the double boiler or use a new clean bowl. Melt the semisweet chocolate in the top of the double boiler as above, stirring occasionally.

STEP 6

6 Spoon the melted semisweet chocolate on top of the melted white chocolate, then run the tip of a dull knife or the handle end of a teaspoon back and forth through the melted chocolate mixture to form a random "marbled" effect.

STEP 6

7 Transfer the baking sheet to the refrigerator until the chocolate hardens completely, about 1 hour.

8 Remove from the refrigerator and turn the baking sheet over onto a flat surface to remove the chocolate "bark." Using your hands, break the chocolate into whatever size pieces you like.

9 Serve immediately or store in an airtight container for up to 2 weeks.

> The chocolate can also be broken by covering it with a clean kitchen towel and hitting it in several places with the end of a rolling pin or another heavy, blunt object.

STEP 8

PIECE-OF-THE-PIE PECAN BARS

YIELD: Sixteen 2¼-inch squares, serving 12 to 16

INGREDIENTS

CRUST

1½ cups plus 2 tablespoons all-purpose flour

1 tablespoon sugar

½ teaspoon salt

½ cup (1 stick) cold unsalted butter, cut into ½-inch cubes

2 tablespoons vegetable shortening

2 to 3 tablespoons ice water

TOPPING

½ cup (1 stick) unsalted butter

½ cup packed light brown sugar

¼ cup granulated sugar

¼ cup honey

2 cups coarsely chopped pecans

¼ cup heavy cream

1 teaspoon vanilla extract

½ cup semisweet chocolate chips

TOOLS

Sifter • large mixing bowl • measuring cups and spoons • pastry cutter (optional) or fork • 9-inch square nonstick baking dish • plastic wrap • parchment paper or aluminum foil • pie weights or beans or rice for weighting crust • oven mitts or pot holders • wire rack • 2- to 3-quart saucepan • wooden spoon • cutting board • chef's knife

If your family loves pecan pie, tell them to look out because these babies are gonna knock their socks off! They're so rich, you need to cut them into small bars—then watch everybody keep coming back for more! Wrap the bars in plastic wrap for terrific lunchbox or picnic basket treats.

DIRECTIONS

CAUTION 👁 🔪 🔥 🧤

1 To make the crust, sift the flour, sugar, and salt into a large mixing bowl.

2 Add the butter and shortening to the flour mixture. Using a pastry cutter, a fork, or your fingers, work in the butter and shortening until the dough resembles coarse crumbs.

STEP 2

3 Add 2 tablespoons of the ice water and continue to work the dough until it just begins to come together, being careful not to overmix. If the dough seems dry and will not come together into a ball, add the remaining tablespoon of water and work dough just enough to evenly distribute the water.

4 Transfer the dough to a 9-inch square baking dish and press with your fingertips until the dough completely covers the bottom of the dish and is smooth.

STEP 4

5 Cover with plastic wrap and transfer the baking dish to the refrigerator; let it rest for at least 1 hour (and up to overnight) before proceeding.

6 Position rack in center of oven and preheat the oven to 400°F.

7 Remove the prepared pie dish from the refrigerator. Remove the plastic wrap and, using a fork, lightly prick the pastry all over. This is called "docking."

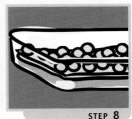
STEP 7

8 Cover the pastry with a piece of parchment paper or aluminum foil, fill with pie weights, and bake the pastry for 15 minutes.

9 Using oven mitts or pot holders, remove the baking dish from the oven and carefully remove the paper and weights. Return the pastry to the oven and continue to bake for another 6 to 8 minutes, or until the pastry is golden brown.

STEP 8

10 Using oven mitts or pot holders, remove the dish from the oven and transfer to a wire rack to cool completely.

11 To make the topping, in a medium saucepan, combine the butter, brown sugar, granulated sugar, and honey.

12 Bring to a boil and cook for 3 minutes. Remove from the heat and stir in the pecans, cream, and vanilla extract.

13 Pour the topping onto the cooled crust, return the baking dish to the oven, and bake until set, about 15 minutes.

14 Using oven mitts or pot holders, remove the dish from the oven and transfer to a wire rack to cool. Scatter the chocolate morsels evenly over the top of the hot pecan mixture. Allow to cool completely before cutting into bars.

> Pie weights are small spheres of metal or porcelain you can buy at cooking supply stores that are used when a pie crust is baked empty. The beauty of pie weights is that you can use them over and over again. If you can't find any, just substitute any type of large dried bean or uncooked rice. But hey, don't try to use the beans or rice in any recipe once they've been baked!

BIG AND CHEWY OATMEAL COOKIES

YIELD: 24 extra-large cookies

INGREDIENTS

1 tablespoon plus 1 teaspoon
   vegetable shortening

1 cup (2 sticks) unsalted butter,
   softened at room temperature

2 cups light brown sugar

2 eggs

1 teaspoon vanilla extract

3 cups old-fashioned oats, not instant
   or quick-cook

1½ cups all-purpose flour

½ teaspoon baking powder

½ teaspoon salt

½ teaspoon cinnamon

¼ teaspoon allspice

¼ teaspoon nutmeg

1½ cups raisins

1 cup chopped walnuts, lightly
   toasted (optional) (page 22)

TOOLS

2 large baking sheets •
measuring cups and spoons
• standing electric mixer
• rubber spatula •
medium mixing bowl •
cutting board
(optional) • chef's
knife (optional) •
spoon (optional) •
oven mitts or pot
holders • wire racks •
metal spatula

These cookies are so big and chewy, one *just might* be enough—especially with a nice tall glass of cold milk. These big boys will keep for several days in an airtight container.

1 Position one oven rack in the center and another in the lower third of the oven and preheat the oven to 375°F.

2 Grease 2 large baking sheets with 2 teaspoons each of the vegetable shortening. Set aside.

3 In the bowl of an electric mixer, cream the butter and brown sugar together at medium speed until very light and fluffy, about 2 to 3 minutes.

4 Turn the mixer off before adding the eggs and vanilla extract, then beat until thoroughly combined.

5 In a medium mixing bowl, combine the oats, flour, baking powder, salt, cinnamon, allspice, and nutmeg and stir to combine.

6 With the mixer turned off, add the dry ingredients to the mixing bowl. Beat on low speed until dry ingredients are just combined, about 1 minute. Turn the mixer off.

7 Add the raisins and walnuts, if desired, and mix at low speed until just combined.

8 Using a ¼-cup measure, scoop the cookie dough into 24 equal portions and place 12 of the dough balls 2 inches apart on each of the prepared baking sheets. Press the dough down slightly with your hands or the back of a spoon.

STEP 8

9 Using oven mitts or pot holders, transfer the baking sheets to the oven and bake for 22 to 25 minutes, exchanging positions of baking sheets after 10 minutes.

10 Using oven mitts or pot holders, remove the baking sheets from the oven and set aside on wire racks for about 10 minutes, or until the cookies are almost completely cooled. Remove the sheets from the racks.

11 Using a metal spatula, transfer the cookies from the baking sheets to the wire racks to allow them to finish cooling. Be careful—these cookies are fragile while they're warm.

BASICALLY BUTTERY COOKIES

YIELD: Eighteen 4-inch cookies

INGREDIENTS

1 cup (2 sticks) unsalted butter, softened at room temperature

$\frac{1}{3}$ cup plus $4\frac{1}{2}$ teaspoons sugar

1 teaspoon vanilla extract

$1\frac{3}{4}$ cups all-purpose flour

Pinch of salt

TOOLS

Standing electric mixer fitted with a paddle attachment • measuring cups and spoons • rubber spatula • plastic wrap • 2 large baking sheets • oven mitts or pot holders • wire racks • metal spatula

This is one of the first basic cookie recipes I ever learned, and they are so delicious you're not going to believe it. But if a simple butter cookie isn't enough of a challenge for you and your family, try drizzling the cookies with melted chocolate as described in the sidebar. You can go all out at holiday time with colored sugars and icings! Everybody in the family can get in on the act.

1. In the bowl of a standing electric mixer fitted with a paddle attachment, cream butter and 1/3 cup of the sugar until very light and fluffy, about 4 minutes.

2. Turn off the mixer and add the vanilla extract, then beat to combine.

3. Turn off the mixer, add the flour and salt, and mix on low speed until the flour is just incorporated. Turn off the mixer.

STEP 1

4. Using a rubber spatula, transfer the dough to a piece of plastic wrap and wrap completely. Refrigerate for 1 hour, or until the dough is cool to the touch and mostly firm.

5. Position one rack in the center and another in the lower third of the oven and preheat the oven to 375°F.

STEP 4

6. Remove the dough from the refrigerator and, using your hands, make 18 walnut-sized balls of dough, about 2 tablespoons each. Divide these evenly between the baking sheets, 3 inches apart, and press down on each cookie to form a slightly flattened disk.

7. Sprinkle 1/4 teaspoon of the sugar evenly over the top of each cookie.

8. Using oven mitts or pot holders, transfer the baking sheets to the oven and bake until cookies are golden brown around the edges, about 16 to 18 minutes, exchanging positions of baking sheets after 8 minutes.

STEP 6

9. Using oven mitts or pot holders, remove the baking sheets from the oven and set on wire racks to cool completely before removing the cookies from the baking sheets with a metal spatula. Be careful—these cookies are fragile while they're warm.

10. Cookies will keep for several days if kept in an airtight container.

If you'd like to kick these up, try this: Melt 1/3 cup of semisweet chocolate morsels in a double boiler or in the microwave. Dip a fork into the melted chocolate and drizzle the chocolate evenly all over the tops of the cooled cookies in a lacy pattern. Allow them to sit until the chocolate hardens, then serve.

MISS HILDA'S POPCORN CAKE

YIELD: 1 cake, serving 12 to 16

INGREDIENTS

¼ cup plus 2 teaspoons vegetable oil

4 quarts (16 cups) plain, unsalted, unbuttered popped popcorn

2 cups M&M candies

1 cup lightly salted cocktail peanuts

½ cup (1 stick) unsalted butter

1 pound marshmallows (mini or regular)

TOOLS

Large tube or Bundt cake pan • measuring cups and spoons • large mixing bowl • medium saucepan • wooden spoon • aluminum foil • oven mitts or pot holders

Here's something great that my mom, Miss Hilda, used to make for me when I was a kid. It's out of this world and you can change it around to suit your tastes. Instead of plain, you can use peanut M&Ms, or the new dulce de leche flavored ones. You can also add chocolate chips or substitute almonds for the peanuts—let everybody in your family choose their favorite!

1 Grease a large tube or Bundt cake pan with 2 teaspoons of the oil. Set aside.

2 In a large bowl, mix the popped corn with the M&Ms and the peanuts and set aside.

3 In a medium saucepan, melt the butter, the remaining $\frac{1}{4}$ cup vegetable oil, and the marshmallows over medium-low heat, stirring occasionally. When melted, use oven mitts or pot holders to remove saucepan from heat and pour marshmallows over the popcorn mixture. Stir to combine.

4 Spoon mixture into the prepared cake pan. Using your hands or the back of a spoon, press firmly so that the mixture is compacted.

STEP 4

5 Cover with aluminum foil to keep moist. Let sit for about 3 to 4 hours, or until firm and set.

6 To serve, invert the cake pan onto a large plate or platter. Shake gently to release the cake. Serve at room temperature.

185

JUST-CHILLIN' CHOCOLATE FRIDGE PIE

YIELD: One 9-inch pie, serving 8 to 10

INGREDIENTS

16 Oreo cookies (either regular or chocolate-filled works just fine)

2 tablespoons melted and cooled unsalted butter

1/2 cup semisweet chocolate morsels

1 (14-ounce) can sweetened condensed milk

1/4 teaspoon salt

2 egg yolks

1/4 cup hot milk

1 teaspoon vanilla extract

1 3/4 cups heavy cream, chilled

2 teaspoons confectioners' sugar

Cocoa powder for dusting (optional)

TOOLS

Food processor • large resealable plastic food storage bag and rolling pin (optional) • 2 medium mixing bowls • small saucepan • measuring cups and spoons • wooden spoon • 9-inch pie pan • oven mitts or pot holders • wire rack • heavy 3 1/2-quart saucepan • can opener • small mixing bowl • whisk • fine-mesh sieve • rubber spatula • plastic wrap • large mixing bowl • electric mixer • sifter (optional)

This is a deliciously creamy chocolate lover's dream! The Oreo cookies add a crispy crunch to the smooth chocolate mousse–like filling. Just make sure to prepare this well enough in advance so that the filling "sets up" properly, and keep in mind that this pie can't be out of the refrigerator for long. That's never a problem in my house!

DIRECTIONS   CAUTION

1 Position rack in center of oven and preheat the oven to 350°F.

2 Chill a large mixing bowl and the beaters of your electric mixer in the freezer until ready to use.

3 In the bowl of a food processor, process cookies until fine crumbs form, following the safety directions on pages 6–7. Or, you can seal the cookies in a large resealable plastic food storage bag and crush with a rolling pin.

4   Transfer the crumbs to a medium mixing bowl and add the melted and cooled butter. Mix thoroughly with a wooden spoon until mixture resembles wet sand.

5   Transfer the mixture to a 9-inch pie pan and, with clean hands, press the mixture evenly along the bottom and up the sides of the pan.

STEP 5

6   Using oven mitts or pot holders, place the pie pan in the oven and bake the crust for 15 minutes. Using oven mitts or pot holders, remove from the oven, transfer to a wire rack, and let cool completely before filling.

7   Meanwhile, in a heavy saucepan over medium heat, melt the chocolate with the condensed milk and salt, stirring until very thick and bubbly, about 5 minutes.

8   Place the egg yolks in a small mixing bowl and whisk in the $\frac{1}{4}$ cup hot milk.

9   Working quickly, add the egg-yolk mixture to the melted chocolate mixture and whisk to combine. Continue to cook until the mixture is very thick and bubbly, about 1 minute.

10 Set a fine-mesh sieve over a second medium mixing bowl and strain the chocolate mixture into the bowl, pressing with a rubber spatula to force the mixture through the sieve if necessary. Discard any lumps.

STEP 10

11 Stir in the vanilla extract and set mixture aside to cool for 15 minutes, stirring occasionally. Place a piece of plastic wrap directly onto the surface of the chocolate mixture and transfer to the refrigerator. Chill thoroughly, about 30 to 45 minutes.

12 In the chilled mixing bowl, using the chilled beaters, beat 1 cup of the heavy cream until stiff peaks form (page 20).

13 Using a rubber spatula, gently fold the whipped cream into the chocolate mixture.

14 Use the spatula to gently transfer the chocolate mixture to the prepared cookie crust, smoothing the top with the spatula.

STEP 13

15 Refrigerate until thoroughly set, at least 3 hours and up to overnight.

16 When ready to serve the pie, combine the remaining $\frac{3}{4}$ cup of heavy cream with the confectioners' sugar in a small bowl and beat with the electric mixer until stiff peaks form. Serve a dollop of whipped cream on top of every slice of pie.

17 Place a small amount of cocoa powder in a sifter and sprinkle over the top of the pie for additional wowing power, if desired.

STEP 17

OPTIONAL GARNISHES
Fresh strawberries   Chocolate curls
Fresh mint leaves   Chopped nuts

LEMON ICEBOX PIE

YIELD: One 9-inch pie, serving 8 to 10

INGREDIENTS

1½ cups graham cracker crumbs

1¼ cups sugar

4 tablespoons (½ stick) melted unsalted butter

2 (14-ounce) cans sweetened condensed milk

1 cup fresh lemon juice

2 large eggs, separated (page 18)

4 large egg whites

Fresh mint sprigs and/or lemon slices for garnish (optional)

TOOLS

2 medium mixing bowls • measuring cups and spoons • wooden spoon • small saucepan • 9-inch pie pan • oven mitts or pot holders • wire rack • can opener • juicer (optional) • whisk • large mixing bowl • electric mixer • rubber spatula • dull knife • can opener

Iceboxes were the very first refrigerators. They were really just big metal boxes with chunks of ice inside to keep things cold. Well, this pie is an old-fashioned dessert from the time when iceboxes were still used, and like they say, it's hard to improve on a good thing. Have a bite and you'll see what I mean.

1. Position rack in center of oven and preheat the oven to 350°F.

2. In a medium bowl, mix together the graham cracker crumbs, 1/2 cup of the sugar, and the melted butter until the mixture resembles wet sand.

3. With clean hands, firmly press the mixture across the bottom and up the sides of a 9-inch pie pan.

STEP 3

4. Using oven mitts or pot holders, place pie pan in oven and bake until the crust is brown and firm, about 15 minutes.

5. Using oven mitts or pot holders, carefully remove the pie crust from the oven and let cool completely on a wire rack before filling.

6. In a separate bowl, whisk together the condensed milk, lemon juice, and egg yolks. Pour into the cooled pie shell.

7. Using oven mitts or pot holders, place pie in oven and bake until set, about 15 minutes. Remove from the oven using oven mitts or pot holders and transfer to a wire rack to cool. Turn off the oven.

8. While the pie is baking, make the meringue by placing the 6 egg whites in a large clean bowl and beating them with an electric mixer until soft peaks start to form (page 20).

9. Slowly add the remaining 3/4 cup of sugar while beating constantly. Beat until stiff, glossy peaks form. Be careful not to overbeat the meringue, as it will appear grainy or clumpy instead of smooth and glossy and will be difficult to spread.

10. Using a rubber spatula, spread the meringue evenly over the warm pie filling, smoothing out to the edges so the meringue won't pucker or get runny during baking.

STEP 10

11. With a dull knife, make decorative peaks in the meringue.

12. Using oven mitts or pot holders, position rack in the upper third of oven and preheat the broiler. If your broiler is separate from your oven, have an adult show you how to use it.

13. Using oven mitts or pot holders, place the pie under the broiler and cook until the meringue is golden brown, about 1 minute. Make sure to keep an eye on this—it will brown quickly!

STEP 11

14. With oven mitts or pot holders, very carefully remove the pie from under the broiler. Refrigerate until thoroughly chilled, at least 2 hours.

15. Serve garnished with a sprig of mint and/or a lemon slice if desired.

> If you're not sure when the meringue is stiff enough, turn off the mixer and remove the beaters from the meringue. If they leave glossy, peaked mounds when lifted then the meringue is done.

VERY STRAWBERRY SHORTCAKE

YIELD: 8 servings

INGREDIENTS

2 pounds fresh strawberries, washed, patted dry, hulled (page 16), and quartered

1/2 cup plus 1 tablespoon sugar

2 tablespoons water

1 teaspoon grated orange zest

1 recipe Totally-from-Scratch Biscuits (page 30), baked with the exception noted in step 4 at right

1 1/2 cups Real Whipped Cream (page 44—you'll need to make 1 1/2 batches)

TOOLS

Large mixing bowl • box grater • cutting board • paring knife • measuring cups and spoons • plastic wrap • oven mitts or pot holders • wire racks • fork (optional)

Perhaps the most all-American dessert, this cake makes a wonderful end to a summer day spent in the sun or for a Fourth of July celebration. It's a good one to make together with family or friends—just make sure you whip the cream immediately before serving, so that it stays nice and fluffy.

1. Position rack in center of oven and preheat the oven to 475°F.

2. Macerate the strawberries by combining the strawberries, ½ cup of the sugar, water, and orange zest in a large bowl (see sidebar below). Stir well to combine.

3. Cover with plastic wrap and refrigerate until the strawberries have softened and given up their juices and mixture is chilled, about 1 hour.

4. While the strawberries are chilling, make the Totally-from-Scratch Biscuits with the following exception: In step 7 on page 31, after brushing the tops of the biscuits with butter, sprinkle the tops with the remaining 1 tablespoon of sugar before baking. Bake as instructed.

5. When the biscuits are done, using oven mitts or pot holders, remove them from the oven and transfer to wire racks to cool. The shortcakes can be served warm or at room temperature.

6. To assemble the shortcakes: Using a knife or fork, split the biscuits in half horizontally and place the bottom halves on each of 8 plates.

7. Spoon ½ cup of the macerated strawberries on each bottom half. Top each serving with 3 tablespoons of Real Whipped Cream (page 44). Lean a biscuit top against each bottom and serve.

STEP 7

> "Macerate" means to soften or steep. You macerate fruit mostly by mixing it with sugar—a chemical reaction causes the berries to give up their good juices.

NEW ORLEANS–STYLE BREAD PUDDING WITH CHOCOLATE SAUCE

YIELD: 10 to 12 servings

INGREDIENTS

8 cups day-old white bread, such as French or Italian, cut into 1-inch cubes (toast if fresh)

5 tablespoons unsalted butter

2 cups heavy cream

2 cups milk

4 large eggs

1 cup light brown sugar

1/2 cup granulated sugar

1/2 cup raisins (optional)

1 tablespoon vanilla extract

2 teaspoons ground cinnamon

1/4 teaspoon ground nutmeg

3 cups Real Whipped Cream (page 44—you'll need to make a triple batch) (optional)

TOOLS

Cutting board • serrated bread knife • large mixing bowl • small saucepan • measuring cups and spoons • rubber spatula • 9 x 13-inch baking dish or casserole • medium mixing bowl • whisk • wooden spoon • oven mitts or pot holders • wire rack

CHOCOLATE SAUCE

YIELD: 3 cups

INGREDIENTS

1 1/2 cups semisweet chocolate morsels

1 cup milk

1 cup heavy cream

2 tablespoons light brown sugar

1/4 teaspoon ground cinnamon

TOOLS

Medium mixing bowl • medium saucepan • measuring cups and spoons • whisk • oven mitts or pot holders

When I moved to New Orleans, one of the first dishes I learned to make was bread pudding. This is my version, with you in mind. The kids can help tear up the bread pieces while the adults work on the sauce. You're gonna love that chocolate drizzled over the top . . . talk about kicking it up a notch!

1. Place the cubed bread in a large mixing bowl.

2. In a small saucepan, melt 4 tablespoons of the butter over medium heat and pour the butter over the bread cubes. Using a rubber spatula, toss to evenly distribute the butter.

3. Grease a 9 by 13-inch baking dish with the remaining 1 tablespoon of butter and set aside.

4. In a medium mixing bowl, combine the cream, milk, eggs, brown sugar, granulated sugar, raisins, if using, vanilla extract, cinnamon, and nutmeg and whisk to combine.

5. Pour the cream mixture over the bread cubes and stir to combine. Let sit for 30 to 45 minutes, or until the bread is soft and has absorbed most of the liquid.

STEP 5

6. Position rack in center of oven and preheat the oven to 350°F.

7. Transfer the bread mixture to the prepared baking dish and bake, uncovered, until the top is golden brown and crispy and the pudding is firm in the center, about 45 minutes.

8. While the bread pudding is baking, prepare the Chocolate Sauce (below).

9. Using oven mitts or pot holders, remove the bread pudding from the oven and set aside on a wire rack to cool for at least 15 minutes before serving.

10. Serve warm with Chocolate Sauce and a triple batch of Real Whipped Cream (page 44), if desired.

CHOCOLATE SAUCE

1. Place the chocolate morsels in a medium mixing bowl and set aside.

2. Combine the milk, cream, brown sugar, and cinnamon in a medium saucepan over medium-high heat and bring just to a boil.

3. Using oven mitts or pot holders, remove the saucepan from the heat immediately and carefully pour the milk mixture over the chocolate morsels. Let sit for one minute, then whisk until smooth.

4. Set aside until ready to serve the bread pudding.

HAZELNUTTY NUGGETS

YIELD: About 12 cups of nuggets

INGREDIENTS

1 (13-ounce jar) Nutella chocolate-hazelnut spread

6 tablespoons (3/4 stick) unsalted butter

6 ounces semisweet chocolate chips

1 (12-ounce) box Crispix cereal

2 1/2 cups confectioners' sugar, for dusting

3/4 cup unsweetened cocoa powder, for dusting

TOOLS

Medium saucepan • measuring cups and spoons • large mixing bowl • wooden spoon • sifter • oven mitts or pot holders

I bet you didn't know that your family's breakfast cereal can make one seriously chocolicious dessert! Kids love making this treat. Make a batch of this when you have lots of friends coming over, or give it as presents for the holidays.

1. In a medium saucepan, melt the Nutella, butter, and chocolate chips over medium-low heat, stirring occasionally. Remove from the heat.

2. Place the Crispix in a large bowl and pour the melted chocolate mixture over the top. Gently stir well to coat evenly.

3. Combine the confectioners' sugar and cocoa in a sifter and sift over the nuggets. Toss to coat evenly. Store in an airtight container.

STEP 2

STEP 3

CANDY-BAR-STUFFED BAKED APPLES

YIELD: Makes 4 servings

INGREDIENTS

4 medium apples (7 to 8 ounces each)

1/4 cup coarsely chopped Skor candy bar

1/4 cup coarsely chopped Snickers candy bar

2 tablespoons unsalted butter

1/4 cup finely chopped Skor candy bar

1/4 cup finely chopped Snickers candy bar

3/4 cup apple cider

1 tablespoon sugar

TOOLS

Cutting board • chef's knife • apple corer or melon baller • 9-inch square baking dish • measuring cups and spoons • small bowl • whisk • oven mitts or pot holders • spoon

This is a great treat to make just after Halloween, when you have all sorts of candy bars left over. I usually make them with Red or Golden Delicious apples, but any variety will do. My favorite candy bars to use are Skor and Snickers, but maybe you kids will get extra-creative. Want to make these over-the-top? While the apples are still warm, place a big scoop of vanilla ice cream on top and dive in!

1. Position rack in center of oven and preheat the oven to 350°F.

2. Place the apples on a cutting board. With a sharp knife, carefully cut the top ½-inch from each apple.

3. Using an apple corer or a small melon baller, scoop out the stem, core, and seeds from each apple, leaving the bottom intact (pages 15–16).

4. Stand the apples in a 9-inch square baking dish, cut side up.

5. Divide the coarsely chopped candy bars among the apples, about 2 tablespoons of candy per apple.

6. Place 1½ teaspoons of the butter inside each apple, on top of the candy bar pieces.

7. Divide the finely chopped candy bars among the apples, about 2 tablespoons of candy per apple.

8. In a small bowl, whisk together the cider and sugar and pour the cider mixture over and around the apples.

9. Using oven mitts or pot holders, place the baking dish in the oven and bake the apples uncovered until tender, about 1 hour and 20 minutes.

10. Using oven mitts or pot holders, carefully remove the apples from the oven and let sit for 5 minutes.

11. Serve hot or warm, spooning the pan juices over the apples, and add vanilla ice cream if desired.

STEP 2

STEP 3

STEP 5

WARNING: These apples are very hot when coming out of the oven, and there is a lot of hot juice. Be careful not to spill any on you!

CAUTION

197

PURE AND SIMPLE CREAM PUFFS

YIELD: 24 puffs, serving 8 to 12

INGREDIENTS

2 large eggs plus 1 large egg white (page 18)

5 tablespoons unsalted butter, cut into small pieces

1/2 cup whole milk

1 1/2 teaspoons granulated sugar

1/4 teaspoon salt

1/2 cup plus 2 tablespoons unbleached all-purpose flour, sifted

3 to 4 cups Real Whipped Cream (page 44—you'll need to make 3-4 batches)

Confectioners' sugar or melted chocolate (page 22) for garnish (optional)

TOOLS

12 x 18-inch baking sheet • parchment paper • small bowl • whisk • 3 1/2-quart saucepan • measuring cups and spoons • wooden spoon • food processor • rubber spatula • pastry bag fitted with a 1/2-inch plain tip • teaspoon • oven mitts or pot holders • knife • small spoon • sifter • cutting board

This is one of the first things I learned to cook in cooking school. Keep in mind that once you master the little puffs, you can fill them with anything your heart desires—jams, jellies, chocolate spreads, and so on. If you fill them with ice cream, then they're called profiteroles. Kids—you're gonna love filling these up.

1. Position rack in center of oven and preheat the oven to 425°F. Line a 12 by 18-inch baking sheet with parchment paper and set aside.

2. In a small bowl, whisk together the eggs and egg white until well combined and frothy. Set aside.

3. Place the butter, milk, sugar, and salt in a saucepan and set over medium heat until the butter melts and the sugar has dissolved, about 3 minutes.

4. Once the milk mixture comes to a boil, remove the pan from the heat and, working quickly, add all of the flour to the saucepan at once. Use a wooden spoon to vigorously stir the flour into the milk and return the pan to the stove.

5. Continue to cook the dough for 2½ to 3 minutes, stirring constantly, until it becomes shiny and forms a ball that comes away from the sides of the pan.

6. Place the dough in a food processor and pulse for 15 to 20 seconds to allow the dough to cool slightly, following the safety directions on pages 6–7.

7. While the machine is still running, slowly drizzle the whisked eggs into the dough by pouring the eggs through the feed tube of the food processor. Be careful here.

(continued)

STEP 7

8. When all of the egg mixture has been added to the dough, turn the processor off and, using a rubber spatula, scrape the dough from the sides of the processor. Replace the lid and and pulse to incorporate.

9. Turn the processor off and carefully remove the blade. Use a spoon to transfer the dough into a pastry bag fitted with a ½-inch plain tip.

STEP 9

10. Pipe the dough into 1¼- to 1½-inch mounds on the prepared baking sheet, about 1 to 1¼ inches apart. You should be able to fit 24 mounds on the sheet.

11. Using the back of a teaspoon dipped in cool water, smooth and reshape the surface of the mounds to form smooth balls.

STEP 10

12. Using oven mitts or pot holders, place the baking sheet in the oven and bake for 15 minutes. Do not open oven door.

STEP 11

13 Without opening the door, reduce the oven temperature to 375°F and continue to bake the cream puffs until golden brown, about 8 to 10 more minutes.

14 Using oven mitts or pot holders, remove the baking sheet from the oven and make a small slit in the side of each puff.

STEP 14

15 Using oven mitts or pot holders, return the baking sheet to the oven and turn the oven off. Crack open the oven door slightly, using a wooden spoon to hold the door open if necessary. Allow the puffs to "dry" in the oven for 45 minutes, undisturbed.

STEP 15

16 Once cool, the puffs should either be used right away or placed in an airtight, nonporous container to be frozen for up to one month. If frozen, they can be thawed in the refrigerator and re-crisped in a preheated 300°F oven for 8 to 10 minutes when you are ready to use them.

17 Fill the puffs by slicing them in half horizontally just below the center. Using a small spoon, gently spoon about 2 to 3 tablespoons of Real Whipped Cream (page 44) into the bottom of the puff. Replace the top of the puff and repeat with the remaining puffs.

STEP 17

18 Sprinkle the tops with sifted confectioners' sugar or drizzle with melted chocolate (page 22), as desired, and serve immediately.

MY FIRST WATERMELON GRANITA

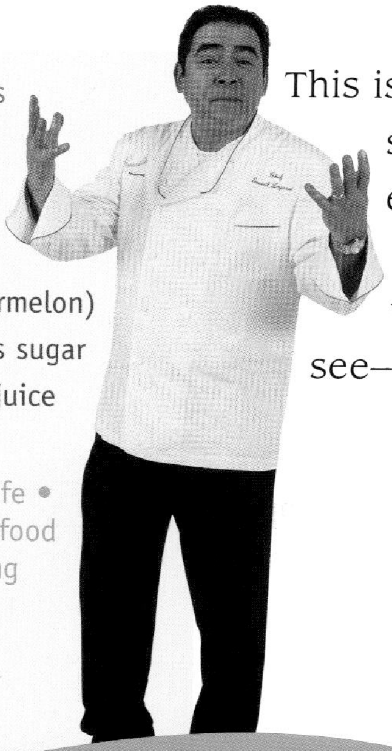

YIELD: 6 to 8 servings

INGREDIENTS

5 cups peeled and
seeded watermelon
chunks (from about a
3-pound slice of watermelon)

1/2 cup plus 2 tablespoons sugar

2 tablespoons fresh lime juice

TOOLS

Cutting board • chef's knife •
paring knife • blender or food
processor • medium mixing
bowl • juicer (optional) •
wooden spoon • fork

This is the first granita I ever made, way back when. I still remember how excited I was to see how easy and fun it was to make this delicious frozen dessert, similar to a sorbet or Italian ice, without any special machines or gadgets. You'll see—it's like a little bit of magic.

1. Place the watermelon chunks in the bowl of a blender or a food processor, replace the top, and blend on high speed until very smooth. Turn the blender off.

2. Transfer the watermelon puree to a mixing bowl and add the sugar and lime juice.

3. Stir with a wooden spoon until the sugar is completely dissolved, about 2 to 3 minutes.

4. Transfer the mixing bowl to the freezer and freeze for 30 minutes.

5. Remove the bowl from the freezer and use a fork to scrape any ice crystals from the sides of the bowl. Stir to incorporate the crystals. Return to the freezer.

STEP 5

6. Repeat this scraping procedure every 30 minutes, or until the consistency is "snowy" when scraped with a fork or spoon, at least 4 hours. Then scoop into bowls or dessert glasses and serve.

EMERIL'S RESTAURANT GUIDE

EMERIL'S TCHOUP CHOP
at Universal Orlando's Royal Pacific Resort
6300 Hollywood Way
Orlando, FL 32819
(407) 503–CHOP (2467)

EMERIL'S ATLANTA
One Alliance Center
3500 Lenox Road
Atlanta, GA 30326
(404) 564–5600

EMERIL'S MIAMI BEACH
at Loews Miami Beach Hotel
1601 Collins Avenue
Miami Beach, FL 33139
(305) 695-4550

EMERIL'S NEW ORLEANS
800 Tchoupitoulas Street
New Orleans, LA 70130
(504) 528–9393

NOLA
534 Rue St. Louis
New Orleans, LA 70130
(504) 522–6652

EMERIL'S DELMONICO
1300 St. Charles Avenue
New Orleans, LA 70130
(504) 525–4937

EMERIL'S NEW ORLEANS FISH HOUSE
at the MGM Grand Hotel and Casino
3799 Las Vegas Boulevard South
Las Vegas, NV 89109
(702) 891-7374

DELMONICO STEAKHOUSE
at the Venetian Resort and Casino
3355 Las Vegas Boulevard South
Las Vegas, NV 89109
(702) 414–3737

EMERIL'S ORLANDO
6000 Universal Boulevard
at Universal Studios CityWalk
Orlando, FL 32819
(407) 224–2424

WEBSITE GUIDE

CHEF EMERIL LAGASSE
www.emerils.com

The official website for everything Emeril. Here you will find listings for all his restaurants, shows, and merchandise and in-depth background and insight into Emeril's culinary world, as well as a monthly on-line magazine and recipes. Bam!

FETZER VINEYARDS
www.fetzer.com

An environmentally and socially conscious grower, Fetzer Vineyards produces Emeril's Classics Wines for the home chef.

WATERFORD/WEDGWOOD
www.wcdesigns.com

The world's leading luxury lifestyle group produces Emeril At Home, ageless additions to the home kitchen.

THE EMERIL LAGASSE FOUNDATION
www.emeril.org

The foundation seeks to inspire, mentor, and enable young people to realize their full potential by supporting programs that create developmental and educational opportunities within the communities where Emeril's restaurants operate.

ALL-CLAD COOKWARE
www.emerilware.com

The cookware that Chef Emeril believes in. Here you will find the entire range of Emerilware by All-Clad, from skillets to sauté pans.

B&G FOODS
www.bgfoods.com

If you want to kick up your kitchen a notch, look for Emeril's original spice blends, salad dressings, marinades, hot sauces, and pasta sauces distributed by B&G Foods and available at supermarkets nationwide.

GOOD MORNING AMERICA
http://abcnews.go.com

Wake up to Chef Emeril on Friday mornings on ABC, when he shares his culinary creations with America.

FOOD NETWORK
www.foodtv.com

Log on to the Food Network's site for recipes and scheduling information for *Emeril Live* and *The Essence of Emeril* shows, and ticket information for *Emeril Live*.

HARPERCOLLINS PUBLISHERS
www.harpercollins.com

This informative site offers background on and chapter excerpts from all of Chef Emeril's best-selling cookbooks.

WÜSTHOF KNIVES
www.wusthof.com

Emerilware Knives gift and block sets, made to Emeril's specifications by one of the world's leading manufacturers of quality cutlery.

INDEX

A

acorn squash, sugar-and-spice, 166–67
American cheese, in junior Wellingtons, 134–35
apples:
    candy-bar-stuffed baked, 196–97
    coring, 15-16
artichokes, simply delicious, 168–69
avocado, in guacamole, 97

B

baby bam seasoning, 25
bacon:
    in Bean Town baked beans, 160–61
    in hot and hearty minestrone, 78–79
    in power-packed spinach salad, 66–67
    in simple-but-fabulous stuffing, 164–65
bagel chips, blow-you-away, 98–99
bagels, yes-you-can, 50–51
barbecue sauce, 138–39
basting, 21
BBQ chicken, rainy-day, 138–39
beans:
    Bean Town baked, 160–61
    chickpeas, in mmmm-hmmm hummus, 108–9
    in crunchy corn chip pie, 128–29
    galore salad, 68–69
    in hot and hearty minestrone, 78–79
    in mambo rice "lasagna," 150–53
beef:
    in crunchy corn chip pie, 128–29
    in garlic lovers' pot roast, 122–23
    in junior Wellingtons, 134–35
    in mighty meaty meatloaf, 124–25
    in shepherd's pie, 132–33
    in talk about a taco salad, 72–73
    in totally sloppy Joes, 88–89
biscuits, totally-from-scratch, 30–31
blanching, 21
blueberry "French toast," ooey gooey, 42–43
breads, 48–59
    blow-you-away bagel chips, 98–99
    everyone loves cornbread, 54–55
    fill-'er-up focaccia with roasted veggies, 84–85
    focaccia, anyone?, 56–57
    hot-out-of-the-oven, 52–53
    it's-a-good-morning muffins, 28–29
    in my kinda salad, 64–65
    never-enough dinner rolls, 48–49
    in one-stop breakfast casserole, 40–41
    for ooey gooey blueberry "French toast," 42–43
    pudding with chocolate sauce, New Orleans–style, 192–93
    in simple-but-fabulous stuffing, 164–65
    totally-from-scratch biscuits, 30–31
    try it, you'll like it zucchini, 58–59
    yes-you-can bagels, 50–51
    see also sandwiches

breakfast, 28–45
    blueberry sauce, 42–43
    casserole, one-stop, 40–41
    doubly delicious hot chocolate with real whipped cream, 44–45
    egg-stra special omelets, 32–33
    Emeril's favorite fried egg sandwich, 34–35
    fresh berry topping, 36, 39
    it's-a-good-morning muffins, 28–29
    ooey gooey blueberry "French toast," 42–43
    totally-from-scratch biscuits, 30–31
    waffable waffles, 36–38

C

cake(s):
    Miss Hilda's popcorn, 184–85
    very strawberry shortcake, 190–91
    see also desserts
casserole, one-stop breakfast, 40–41
Cheddar cheese:
    in Chef Emeril's salad, 70–71
    in crunchy corn chip pie, 128–29
    in Emeril's con queso, 106–7
    in fries, oven crispy, 100–101
    in nacho fiesta, 94–95
    in one-stop breakfast casserole, 40–41
    in say "cheese" enchiladas, 120–21
    in shepherd's pie, 132–33
    in talk about a taco salad, 72–73
cheese(y):
    in Chef Emeril's salad, 70–71
    in chicken Parmesan Emeril-style, 136–37
    in crunchy corn chip pie, 128–29
    in Emeril's con queso, 106–7
    in fill-'er-up focaccia with roasted veggies, 84–85
    in fondue for you, 104–5
    in fries, oven crispy, 100–101
    in junior Wellingtons, 134–35
    in my kinda salad, 64–65
    in nacho fiesta, 94–95
    in one-stop breakfast casserole, 40–41
    in pizzazy pizza sandwiches, 82–83
    in puff pastry—with a twist, 102–3
    in say "cheese" enchiladas, 120–21
    in scoop-it-up spinach dip, 110–11
    in talk about a taco salad, 72–73
    in very veggie lasagna, 114–15
    see also specific cheeses
chicken:
    Parmesan, Emeril-style, 136–37
    perfect roast, 140–41
    rainy-day BBQ, 138–39
    and rice soup, feel-good, 76–77
    salad sandwiches, check out my, 90–91

chocolate:
    bark with pecans, Megan's white, 176–77
    fridge pie, just-chillin', 186–87
    hot, doubly delicious, with real whipped cream, 44–45
    sauce, New Orleans–style bread pudding with, 192–93
chopping and mincing, 14–15
cocktail sauce, for shrimp, 62–63
con queso, Emeril's, 106–7
cookies and bars:
    basically buttery, 182–83
    big and chewy oatmeal, 180–81
    piece-of-the-pie pecan, 178–79
cooking, 14–25
    kitchen tools for, 8–13
    safety tips, 4–7
    techniques, 19–23
    testing for doneness, 23–24
cornbread, everyone loves, 54–55
corn chip pie, crunchy, 128–29
corn-off-the-cob pudding, 158–59
crabmeat, in Emeril's favorite stuffed shrimp, 148–49
cream, real whipped, 44–45
cream puffs, pure and simple, 198–201

D

desserts, 176–203
    basically buttery cookies, 182–83
    big and chewy oatmeal cookies, 180–81
    candy-bar-stuffed baked apples, 196–97
    hazelnutty nuggets, 194–95
    just-chillin' chocolate fridge pie, 186–87
    lemon icebox pie, 188–89
    Megan's white chocolate bark with pecans, 176–77
    Miss Hilda's popcorn cake, 184–85
    my first watermelon granita, 202–3
    New Orleans–style bread pudding with chocolate sauce, 192–93
    piece-of-the-pie pecan bars, 178–79
    pure and simple cream puffs, 198–201
    very strawberry shortcake, 190–91
dinner, 114–53
    bread 'em and bake 'em pork chops, 130–31
    chicken Parmesan Emeril-style, 136–37
    classic roast turkey, 142–45
    crunchy corn chip pie, 128–29
    Emeril's favorite stuffed shrimp, 148–49
    fettuccine Alfredo my way, 117–18
    fish in a pouch, 146–47
    garlic lovers' pot roast, 122–23
    junior Wellingtons, 134–35
    mambo rice "lasagna," 150–53
    mighty meaty meatloaf, 124–25
    pasta primavera, 118–19
    penne with Italian sausage, 126–27
    perfect roast chicken, 140–41
    rainy-day BBQ chicken, 138–39
    say "cheese" enchiladas, 120–21
    shepherd's pie, 132–33
    very veggie lasagna, 114–15

dip, scoop-it-up spinach, 110–11
dough, cooking with, 18, 21–22

E

eggs, 20, 24
    in corn-off-the-cob pudding, 158–59
    cracking and separating, 18
    egg-stra special omelets, 32–33
    in lemon icebox pie, 188–89
    in New Orleans–style bread pudding, 192–93
    in one-stop breakfast casserole, 40–41
    sandwich, Emeril's favorite fried, 34–35
Emmentaler cheese, in fondue for you, 104–5
enchiladas, say "cheese," 120–21

F

fettuccine Alfredo my way, 116–17
fish in a pouch, 146–47
focaccia:
    focaccia, anyone?, 56–57
    with roasted veggies, fill-'er-up, 84–85
fondue for you, 104–5
food processors, 71
"French toast," ooey gooey blueberry, 42–43
fries, oven crispy cheese, 100–1
fruits, 16–17
    see also specific fruits

G

garlic lovers' pot roast, 122–23
glaze, for mighty meaty meatloaf, 124–25
granita, my first watermelon, 202–3
grating hard foods, 15
gravy, for open-faced roast turkey sandwiches, 86–87
Gruyère cheese, in fondue for you, 104–5
guacamole, 97

H

ham:
    in Chef Emeril's salad, 70–71
    in Emeril's favorite fried egg sandwich, 34–35
hazelnutty nuggets, 194–95
hot chocolate, doubly delicious, with real whipped cream, 44–45
hummus, mmmm-hmmm, 108–9

J

juicing citrus fruits, 16–17

K

kitchen tools, 8–13

L

lamb, in shepherd's pie, 132–33
lasagna:
  mambo rice, 150–53
  very veggie, 114–15
lemon icebox pie, 188–89
lettuce:
  in Chef Emeril's salad, 70–71
  in my kinda salad, 64–65
  in talk about a taco salad, 72–73

M

measurements, 19, 25
meatloaf, mighty meaty, 124–25
Megan's white chocolate bark with pecans, 176–77
minestrone, hot and hearty, 78–79
Monterey Jack cheese:
  in crunchy corn chip pie, 128–29
  in Emeril's con queso, 106–7
  in nacho fiesta, 94–95
  in one-stop breakfast casserole, 40–41
  in scoop-it-up spinach dip, 110–11
  in talk about a taco salad, 72–73
mozzarella cheese:
  in chicken Parmesan Emeril-style, 136–37
  in fill-'er-up focaccia with roasted veggies, 84–85
  in pizzazy pizza sandwiches, 82–83
  in very veggie lasagna, 114–15
muffins, it's-a-good-morning, 28–29
mushrooms:
  in fondue for you, 104–5
  in power-packed spinach salad, 66–67
  sautéed, 86–87

N

nacho fiesta, 94–95
New Orleans–style bread pudding with chocolate sauce, 192–93
nuts:
  in big and chewy oatmeal cookies, 180–81
  in hazelnutty nuggets, 194–95
  in zucchini bread, 58–59
  see also peanuts; pecans

O

oatmeal cookies, big and chewy, 180–81
omelets, egg-stra special, 32–33

P

pancetta, in hot and hearty minestrone, 79
Parmesan cheese:
  in best baked tomatoes, 170–71
  in cheesy puff pastry—with a twist, 102–3
  in chicken Parmesan Emeril-style, 136–37
  in my kinda salad, 64–65
  in pizzazy pizza sandwiches, 82–83
  in scoop-it-up spinach dip, 110–11
  in very veggie lasagna, 114–15

pasta:
  in chicken Parmesan Emeril-style, 136–37
  fettuccine Alfredo my way, 116–17
  penne with Italian sausage, 126–27
  primavera, 118–19
  very veggie lasagna, 114–15
peanuts, in Miss Hilda's popcorn cake, 184–85
peas, minty green, 172–73
pecan(s):
  bars, piece-of-the-pie, 178–79
  in it's-a-good morning muffins, 28–29
  Megan's white chocolate bark with, 176–77
pecorino Romano cheese, in scoop-it-up spinach dip, 110–11
peeling fruits and veggies, 14
penne with Italian sausage, 126–27
pie(s):
  crunchy corn chip, 128–29
  just-chillin' chocolate fridge, 186–87
  lemon icebox, 188–89
  shepherd's, 132–33
pizza sandwiches, pizzazy, 82–83
plantains, in mambo rice "lasagna," 153
popcorn cake, Miss Hilda's, 184–85
pork:
  chops, bread 'em and bake 'em, 130–31
  in mambo rice "lasagna," 150–53
  in mighty meaty meatloaf, 124–25
potatoes:
  for oven crispy cheese fries, 100–1
  in shepherd's pie, 132–33
provolone cheese:
  in fill-'er-up focaccia with roasted veggies, 84–85
  in pizzazy pizza sandwiches, 82–83
puff pastry:
  for cheesy—with a twist, 102–3
  for junior Wellingtons, 134–35

Q

queso blanco cheese, in fill-'er-up focaccia with roasted veggies, 84–85

R

rice:
  feel-good chicken soup with, 76–77
  "lasagna," mambo, 150–53
  pilaf, real-deal, 162–63
rolls, never-enough dinner, 48–49

S

salad dressing:
  for Chef Emeril's salad, 70–71
  for power-packed spinach salad, 66–67

salads, 62–73
  beans galore, 68–69
  catch a shrimp cocktail, 62–63
  Chef Emeril's, 70–71
  my kinda, 64–65
  power-packed spinach, 66–67
  talk about a taco, 72–73
salsa, 96
sandwiches, 34–35, 82–91
  check out my chicken salad, 90–91
  Emeril's favorite fried egg, 34–35
  fill-'er-up focaccia with roasted veggies, 84–85
  open-faced roast turkey, 86–87
  pizzazy pizza, 82–83
  totally sloppy Joes, 88–89
sauce(s):
  barbecue, for rainy-day BBQ chicken, 138–39
  blueberry, for ooey gooey "French toast," 42–43
  chocolate, New Orleans–style bread pudding
     with, 192–93
  cocktail, for shrimp, 62–63
sausage:
  in one-stop breakfast casserole, 40–41
  penne with Italian, 126–27
  removal of casing, 18
seasonings, 24–25
shepherd's pie, 132–33
shortcake, very strawberry, 190–91
shrimp:
  cocktail, catch a, 62–63
  Emeril's favorite stuffed, 148–49
  peeling and deveining, 17
side dishes, 156–73
  Bean Town baked beans, 160–61
  best baked tomatoes, 170–71
  corn-off-the-cob pudding, 158–59
  minty green peas, 172–73
  oven-roasted veggies, 156–57
  real-deal rice pilaf, 162–63
  simple-but-fabulous stuffing, 164–65
  simply delicious artichokes, 168–69
  sugar-and-spice acorn squash, 166–67
sloppy Joes, totally, 88–89
snacks, 94–111
  blow-you-away bagel chips, 98–99
  cheesy puff pastry—with a twist, 102–3
  Emeril's con queso, 106–7
  fondue for you, 104–5
  guacamole, 97
  mmmm-hmmm hummus, 108–9
  nacho fiesta, 94–95
  oven crispy cheese fries, 100–1
  salsa, 96
  scoop-it-up spinach dip, 110–11
soups, 76–81
  feel-good chicken and rice, 76–77
  hot and hearty minestrone, 78–79
  tortellini in brodo, 80–81
spinach:
  dip, scoop-it-up, 110–11
  in fill-'er-up focaccia with roasted veggies, 84–85
  salad, power-packed, 66–67
squash, sugar-and-spice acorn, 166–67

strawberries:
  in fresh berry topping, 36
  in shortcake, very strawberry, 190–91
stuffing, simple-but-fabulous, 164–65
Swiss cheese:
  in Chef Emeril's salad, 70–71
  in one-stop breakfast casserole, 40–41

T

taco salad, talk about a, 72–73
tahini, 109
toasting foods, 22–23
tomatoes:
  best baked, 170–71
  in hot and hearty minestrone, 78–79
  in mambo rice "lasagna," 150–53
  in power-packed spinach salad, 66–67
  in salsa, 96
  in say "cheese" enchiladas, 120–21
  in talk about a taco salad, 72–73
  in very veggie lasagna, 114–15
toppings:
  fresh berry, for waffles, 36, 39
  for piece-of-the-pie pecan bars, 178–79
  for yes-you-can bagels, 50
tortellini in brodo, 80–81
tortillas:
  for say "cheese" enchiladas, 120–21
  for talk about a taco salad, 72–73
turkey:
  in Chef Emeril's salad, 70–71
  classic roast, 142–45
  defrosting, 143
  sandwiches, open-faced roast, 86–87

V

veal, in mighty meaty meatloaf, 124–25
vegetables:
  in hot and hearty minestrone, 78–79
  lasagna, very veggie, 114–15
  oven-roasted veggies, 156–57
  in pasta primavera, 118–19
  roasted, fill-'er-up focaccia with, 84–85
  see also specific vegetables

W

waffles, waffable, 36–38
watermelon granita, my first, 202–3
Wellingtons, junior, 134–35

Z

zesting citrus fruits, 16
zucchini bread, try it, you'll like it, 58–59